Keepsake Cards

Beaded Memories for Special Occasions

Katie Dean

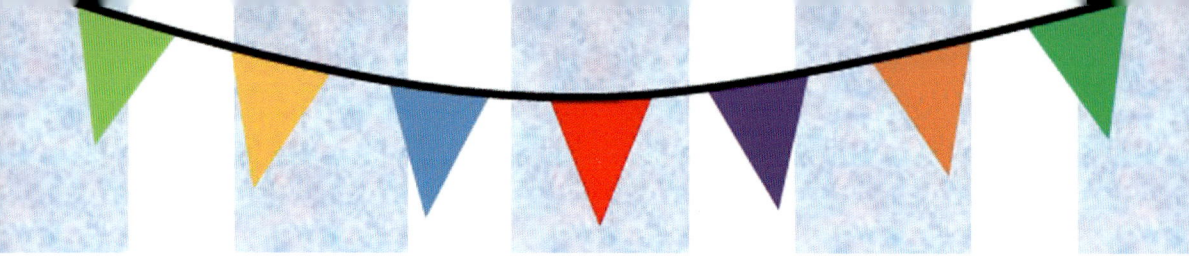

Text and photos (C) Katie Dean 2016. Designs (C) Katie Dean 2013-2016. The written instructions, designs, patterns and projects in this book are intended for the personal use of the reader and may be reproduced for that purpose only. Photocopying, creating electronic copies or printing this book for any commercial use is forbidden under law without the written permission of the copyright holder. You may sell the beaded cards you have made provided you credit Katie Dean as the designer. If you wish to teach Keepsake Cards, you must obtain written permission from Katie Dean.

Every effort has been made to ensure that all the information in this book is accurate. However, due to differing conditions, tools and individual skills, the author and publisher cannot be held responsible for the way in which the projects turn out. Any injuries, losses or other damages that may result from the use of information in this book are the responsibility of the reader.

Any similarity of the designs included in this book to any existing designs is purely coincidental. The Blurb-provided layout designs and graphic elements are copyright Blurb Inc. This book was created using the Blurb creative publishing service.

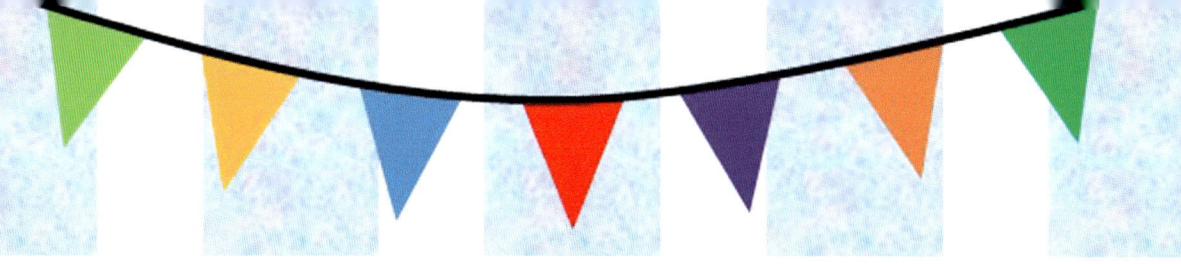

Contents

Introduction 4
A Note on Materials and Techniques 6
Rectangular Card Blanks 8
Landscape Card Blanks 16
Square Card Blanks 20
Square Aperture Cards 32
Card Front Decoration 36
Card Messages 42
Projects 52
Gallery 74
Useful Stuff 80
Biography 82

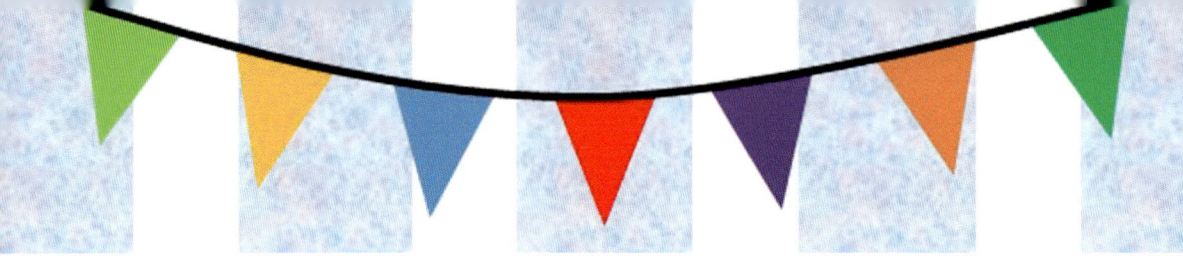

Introduction

I have always enjoyed making beaded gifts that celebrate special occasions. The idea for the Keepsake cards came about when I was asked to make a project to celebrate the 50th issue of Bead Magazine. I realised that it was possible to create different shapes of card and decorate them in a multitude of different ways.

This book is all about allowing you to use your creativity to make something suitable for

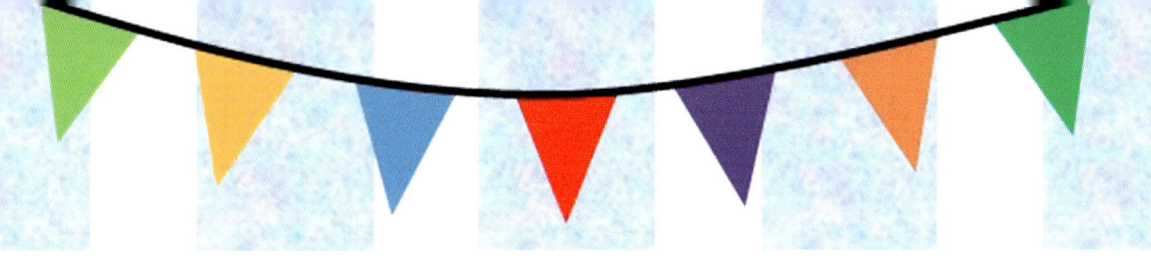

your own celebratory occasion. You will start by learning how to make card blanks in two shapes, then learn how to add a decoration to the front and a message inside. I have included some complete projects for you to try, but there are also separate design ideas that you can mix and match to suit you.

I hope this will give you the chance to explore your creative side and make some truly memorable gifts for friends and relatives.

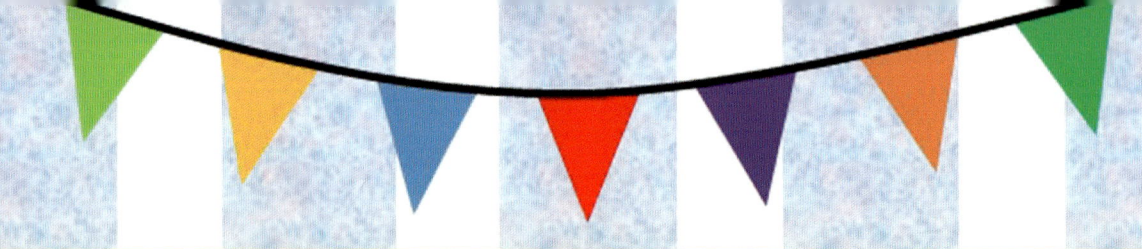

A Note on Materials and Techniques

For all these projects I recommend using Delica beads to make the card blanks. I used both size 11 and size 10. The size 10 will allow you to create a bigger card without stitching more rows! For the text inside the cards, you will want to use size 15 beads (any brand is fine) as this will scale the words down to fit. For the complete projects I have specified which beads to use, but if you are designing your own, you may need to experiment a little. If you know you need specific text, then make that first so that you can then size the card blank to contain the text.

You can use whichever type of thread you prefer. I have used 4lb Fireline as that will fit through all the beads and I find it is strong and helps me to get a good, even tension. For some projects you may also wish to incorporate some of the shaped seed beads (eg Tilas, Superduos) or 3mm or 4mm round or faceted beads. In general, if you try to use beads larger than 4mm, you will find they are out of proportion to the card blanks. In addition to these basic materials, you will need a beading needle, scissors, beading mat and a good light source.

All the card blanks are made using Peyote stitch. The rectangular cards use even and odd count. The square cards use circular Peyote and you will need a tiny bit of the most basic Right Angle Weave. The card decorations are made using a variety of different techniques: Peyote stitch, Brick stitch, Herringbone, Square stitch. I have assumed that you are already familiar with these techniques, but if you need any additional help, you can download free tutorials for all of them from my website, www.beadflowers.co.uk.

In general, I would recommend these projects for people who already have some beading experience, but if you are still learning, please don't be put off. You can learn as you go with these cards. They are projects that you can make in stages and if you are struggling with the terminology or any of the beading basics, you can find blogs to help you at www.myworldofbeads.com.

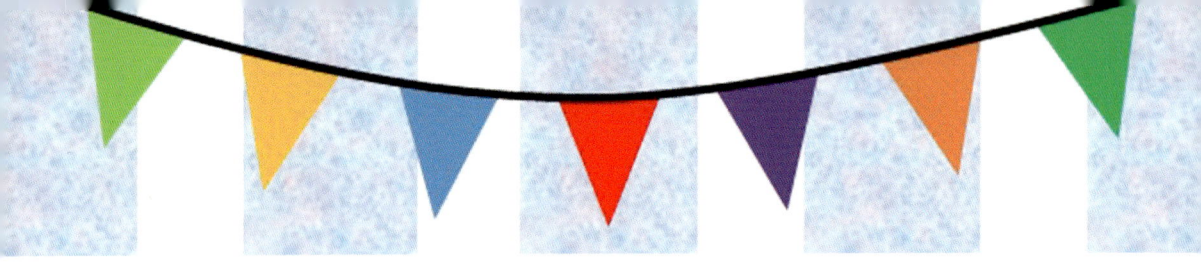

Rectangular Card Blank with Aperture

Inside the Rectangular Card Blank

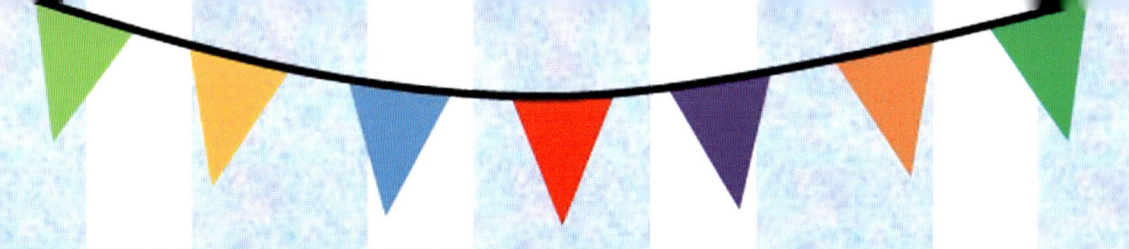

Rectangular Card Blanks

In this chapter you will learn how to create a rectangular card blank with an aperture. If you are used to making cards, then you will be familiar with 'Aperture Card Blanks'. You are going to be creating a beaded version using the same design principles as the paper card blanks.

Use even count Peyote stitch to create a long strip of beadwork, then add the aperture section, working in a combination of odd and even count Peyote. Fold the strip and stitch it to create a card that you can decorate. In order to stiffen the back of the card, add a row of bead quilling to the top and bottom.

Materials
12g size 11 Delicas in main colour (A)
1g size 11 Delicas in accent colour (B)

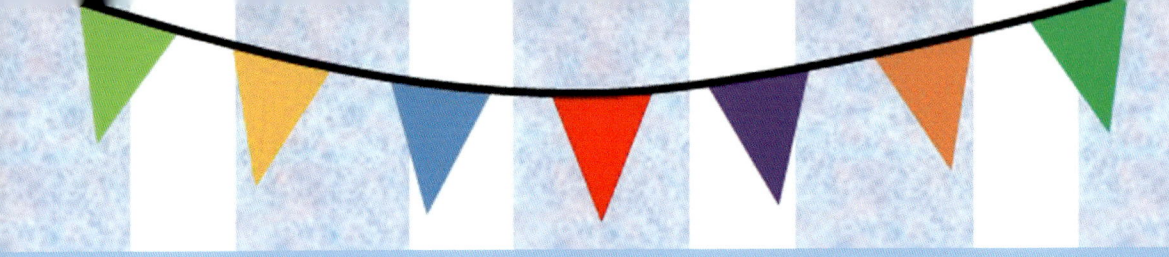

Step 1: Using the (A) beads, stitch a strip of even count Peyote that has 20 beads per row (ie you will start by picking up 40(A) to create rows 1 and 2) and is 92 rows long. This will give the basic front and back to the card. Left-hand diagram shows the first four rows of your Peyote strip.

Step 2: Make the front aperture section. Continue stitching on your strip - add 2 rows using all (A) beads. Add 2 more rows each with 1(A) then 19(B). Stitch 2 rows with19(A) then 1(B). Convert to working in odd count peyote. For the first row, add 2(A). Turn around using your preferred method. In the second row add 1(B). Continue this sequence for another 32 rows forming a small strip up one edge of your card. Leave your thread and put this section to one side. Start a new piece of Peyote, working as follows:

Rows 1 & 2: pick up 40(A)

Rows 3 & 4: work in even count Peyote and add 1(A) and 19(B) in each row

Rows 5 & 6: continue working in even count Peyote and add 19(A) and 1(B) in each row

Convert to the odd count Peyote and work 34 rows in the same way as you did on the first half of the aperture. Zip up the L-shaped section you have just stitched onto the strip to form your aperture. So the odd count strip on each piece will zip onto the other side of the full length strip to complete the frame. See the right-hand diagram.

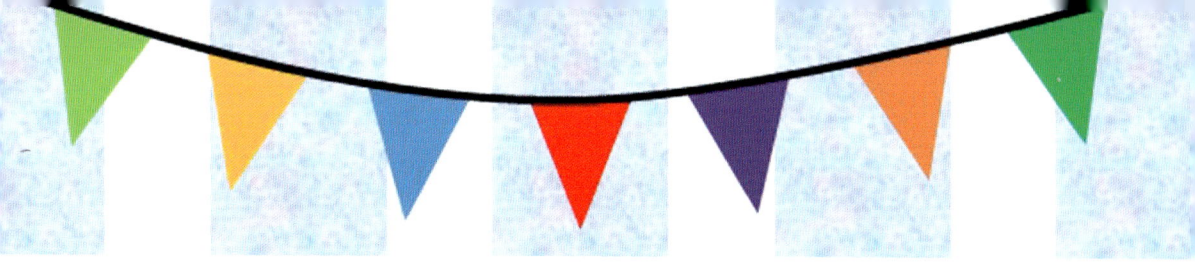

The first four rows of even count Peyote

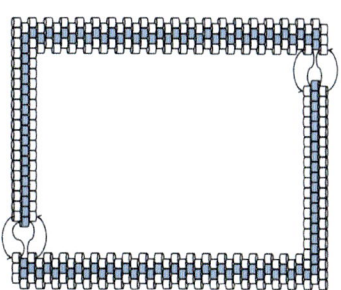

How to join the aperture pieces

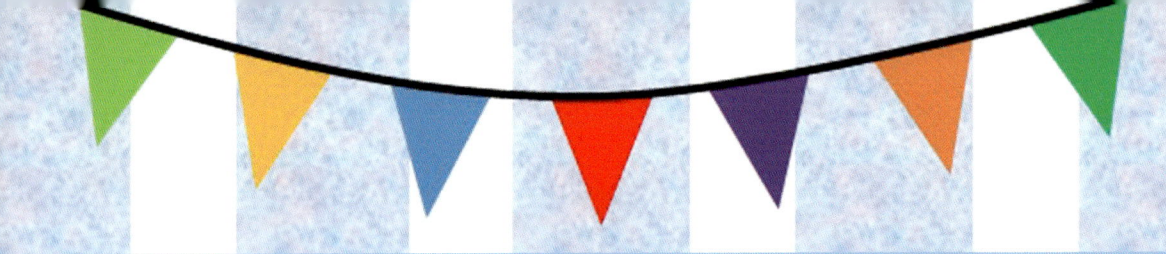

Step 3: fold your beadwork over to form the card and stitch it into place. The initial long strip will form sections (A) and (B) in the left-hand diagram, so this will fold in half. You should be able to zip up the outer edge of the aperture (section (C) in the left-hand diagram) to the middle row of the main section of the card. The line along which you will zip up is the line that divides sections (A) and (B) in the left-hand diagram. If you find this unclear, then reference back to the photos of the card blank on page 8.

Step 4: Join the top and bottom edges of the aperture using an overstitch: pass from an aperture edge bead (pink) down into the card edge bead (yellow), then up through the neighbouring card edge bead, then down through the next aperture edge bead and you are ready to move up through the following aperture edge bead. Repeat this sequence all along the card. See the right-hand diagram. The photo shows the finished join on the card edge. You will notice that the thread is visible, so you may want to use a thread that tones well with your beads for this part of the card assembly.

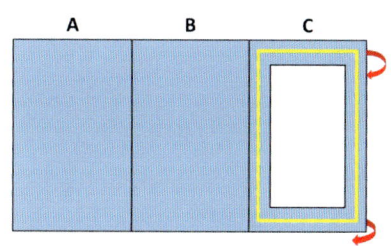
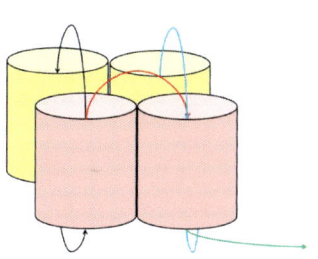

Folding the card and joining the top and bottom edges

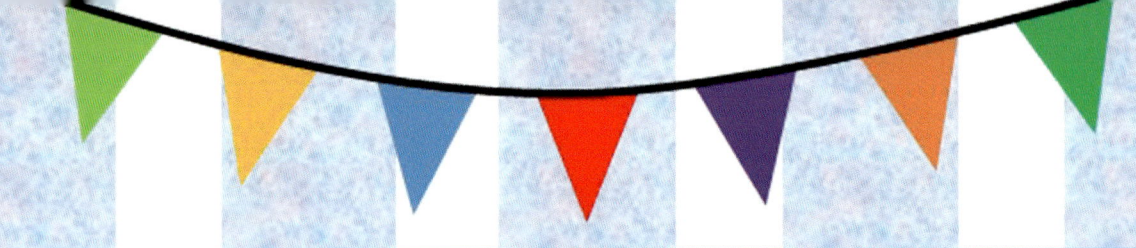

Step 5: stiffen the edges of the card back so that it has sufficient stability to stand up. Begin by stitching an extra row of Peyote along the side of the back, using the (A) beads (blue beads in diagram). Fold this over and zip it up to the row that would have been the third (from the edge - outlined in red in the diagram) in your original card back. See the top diagram and photo.

Step 6: use a version of bead quilling to stiffen the top and bottom of the card. Exit from the end bead in the top (or bottom) row of the card back. Pick up 1(A) and pass into the bead from which you exited. If you exited from the top of the bead, then pass back in from bottom to top. The new bead should now be sitting on top of the end bead on the edge row. See the bottom diagram (new beads are shown in pink, existing card beads in cream).

Step 7: Pass into the adjacent bead in your card edge. If you are exiting from the top, then pass into the adjacent bead from top to bottom. Pick up 1(A) and pass through the bead from which you started, moving from top to bottom. Now pass into the first bead that you added (adjacent to your new bead), working from bottom to top. Pass back into the newest bead, working from top to bottom and then back into the card bead from which you started, working from bottom to top. You should find that each new bead you are adding is joined at top and bottom to both the card bead on which it is sitting and its neighbouring additional bead. See the bottom diagram and photo. If you prefer to use a different thread path to achieve this, then that is fine.

Step 8: keep repeating step 7 until you have added beads all the way along the row. Repeat the same process along the bottom edge of the card.

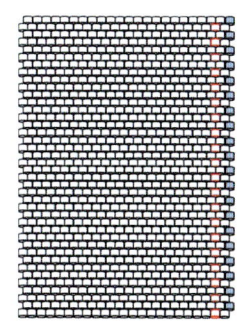

The card back outer edge support

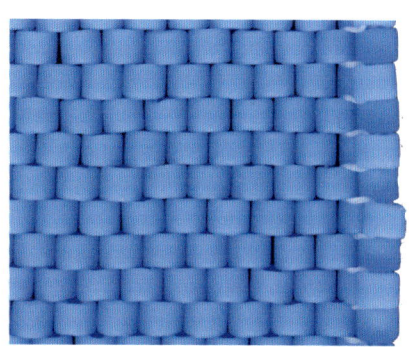

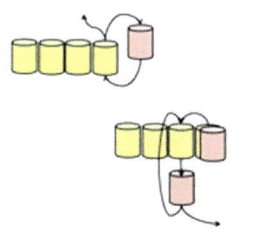

Bead Quilling

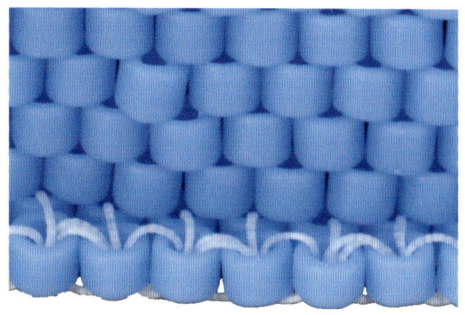

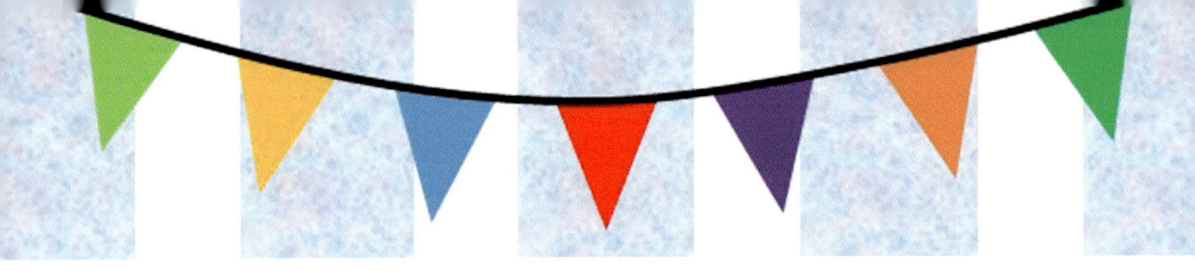

Create a picture inside the aperture

Add text as you make the card blank

Rectangular Landscape Card Blanks

In this chapter you will learn how to create a rectangular card blank with an aperture, an image and a greeting. It is similar to the rectangular blank from the previous section, but results in a card that is entirely double-sided. Your greeting will be aligned in landscape orientation (unless you create a brick stitch alphabet to use!)

Use even count Peyote stitch to create a long strip of beadwork, with three sections, then add the aperture section, working in a combination of odd and even count Peyote. Fold the strip and stitch it to create a card that you can decorate.

Materials

12g size 11 Delicas in main colour (A)
1g size 11 Delicas in accent colour (B)
6g size 11 Delicas in the colours to create your chosen image

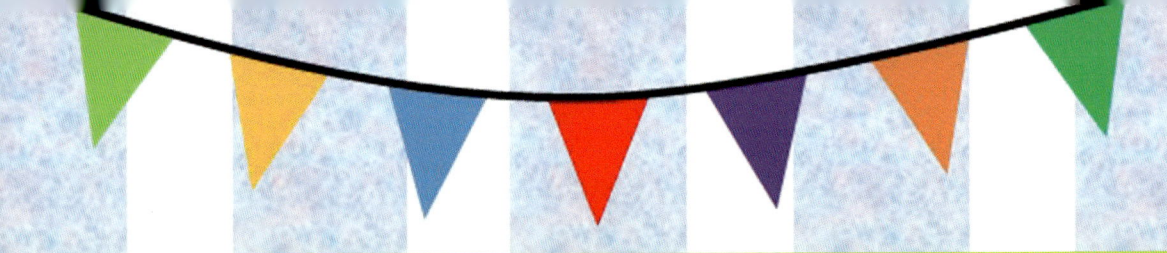

Step 1: Using the size 11 main colour Delicas, stitch a strip of even count Peyote that has 20 beads per row (ie you will start by picking up 40(A) to create rows 1 and 2) and is 46 rows long. This will give the basic back to the card.

Step 2: Stitch another 46 rows that will form your card's greeting. You can use the blank pattern paper (on facing page) to design a greeting. The side that joins onto the card back you have just stitched should be the bottom of your greeting.

Step 3: Continue to stitch another 46 rows that will form the picture. Again, you can use the blank pattern to design your picture. The side that joins onto the card greeting should be the top of your picture, so make sure you get this right.

Step 4: Follow the instructions from the rectangular card blank to add the aperture (page 10) - this will start from the side that forms the bottom of your picture. You should end up with a strip as shown in the diagram - you will have worked from left to right.

Step 5: Fold the card back (section A) behind your greeting (section B) and zip up the first row of the back to the last row of your greeting. Fold the aperture (section D) behind the picture section (C) and zip the edge of the aperture to the first row of the picture. Use the assembly technique described for the rectangular card to join the sides of your card. This completes the card blank, so you can then add some decoration to the front, but you will not need to add a greeting inside.

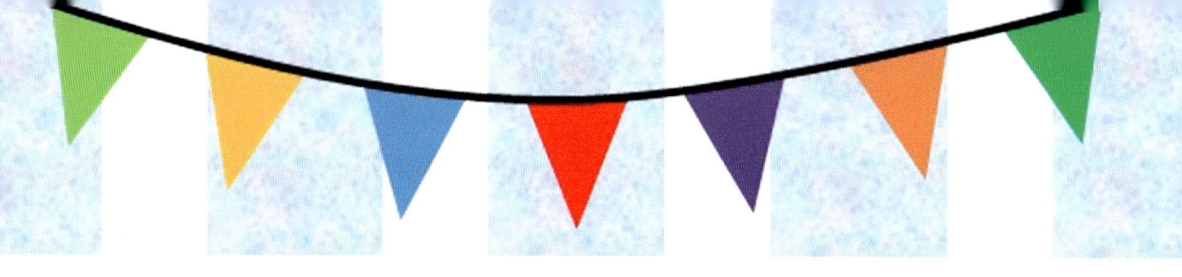

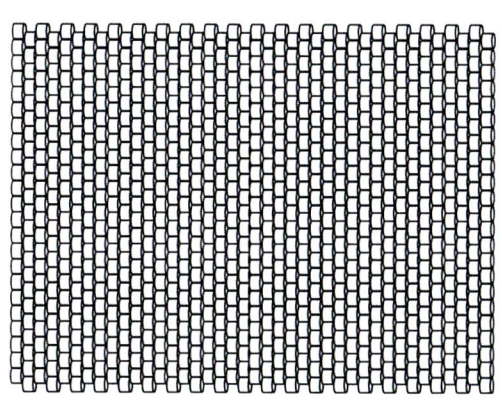

Photocopy and enlarge the pattern paper so you can design your own picture and text

Take care that you stitch the sections in the right order, get the text and picture up the right way and then fold the sections in the right direction.

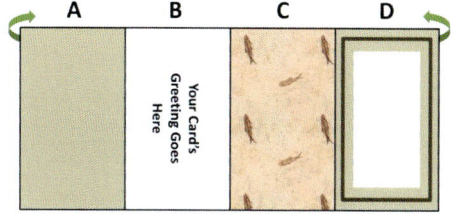

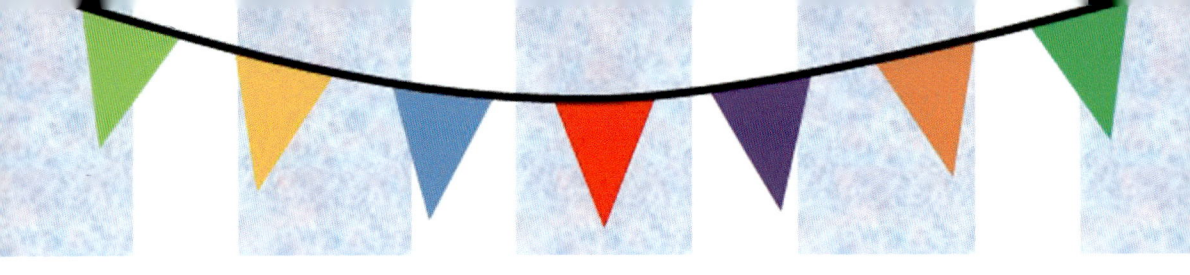

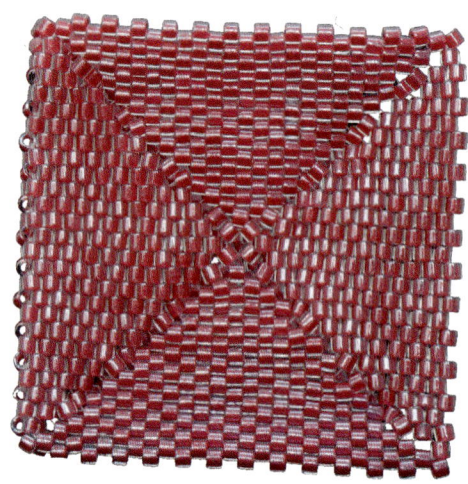

The Square Card Blank

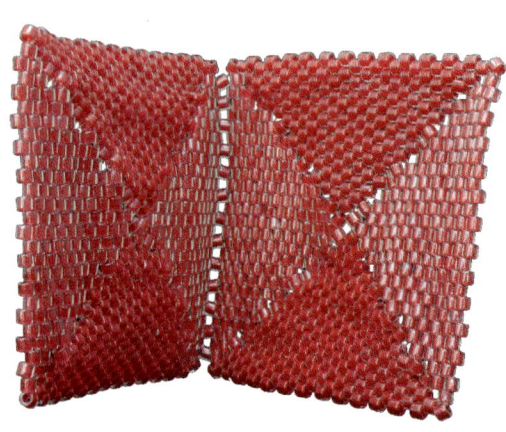

Inside the Square Card Blank

Square Card Blanks

The square shaped card is made using a version of circular Peyote stitch that will give you a square shape. You are basically going to be using a pattern that is established over five rows and then repeats itself every five rows until you have completed the card front. You will then use the same technique to make an identical card back. The two halves of the card are linked using a very basic Right Angle Weave.

Once you have mastered the technique, you can add different designs into your square card blanks.

Materials
13g size 10 Delicas

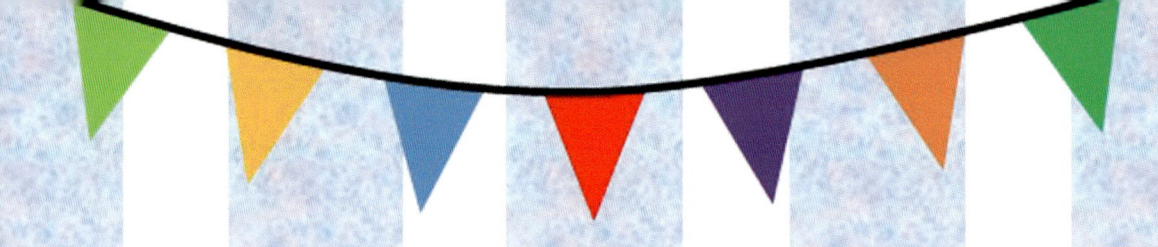

Row 1: Pick up 4 beads and pass through them all again to form a circle. Knot your working and tail threads to hold the circle firm. Pass on through two beads. See figure 1.

Row 2: Pick up 1 bead and pass through the next bead from your circle. Repeat three times, so you will add 1 bead between each of your four beads. After adding the fourth bead, step up to exit from the first bead you added in this row. See figure 2.

Row 3: Pick up 3 beads and pass through the next bead from your previous row. Repeat three more times and then step up by passing through the first bead in your first group of three beads. See figure 3.
Note: this row is the first in the square increase cycle. In each subsequent cycle, you will find you are adding the three beads in each corner of your square, with single beads along the four sides.

Row 4: Pick up 2 beads and pass through the third bead in your group of three. Pick up 1 bead and pass through the first bead in your next group of three. Repeat this sequence three more times to complete the row. At the end of the row, you should step up by passing through the first bead in your first pair of beads. See figure 4.

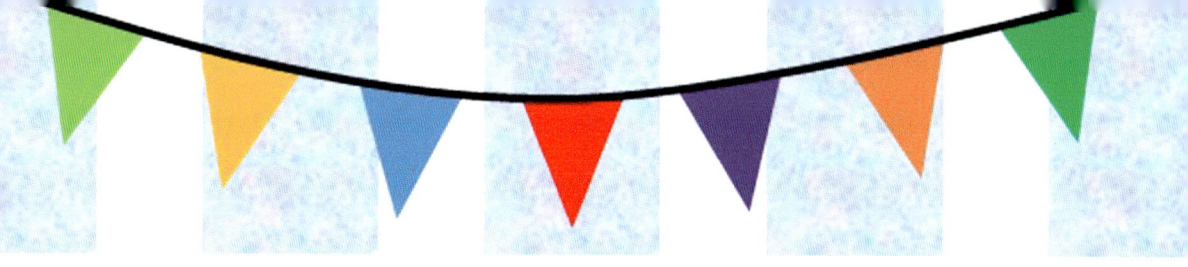

Figure 1

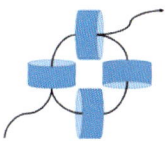

Figure 2

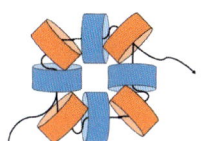

Figure 3

Figure 4

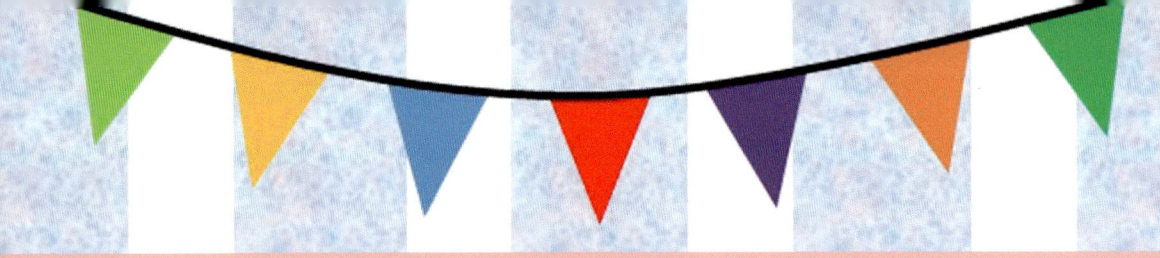

Row 5: Pick up 2 beads and pass through the second bead in your pair. Add a single bead in each of the next two spaces – this will be along the side of your square. You should now be exiting from the first bead in the next pair of beads. Repeat this sequence three more times to complete the row. At the end of the row, step up by passing through the first bead in your first pair of beads. See figure 5.

Row 6: Pick up 1 bead and pass through the second bead in your pair. Add a single bead in each space along the side, so you will end up exiting from the first bead in your next pair. Repeat this sequence three more times to complete the row. See figure 6.

Row 7: Add 1 bead in every space around the row and at the end, step up by passing through the first bead in this row. See figure 7.

Note: this completes your increase cycle. You should see your beads sitting in a clear square shape and you should have a big gap in each corner. This means you are ready to begin the next increase cycle.

Rows 8-12: Repeat rows 3-7 to make a second increase cycle. You should keep the increases in the first three rows in the corner spaces, so this means you might not necessarily be adding beads in the order in which they are stated in the written instructions above. Make sure you remember the step up at the end of every row. See figure 8.

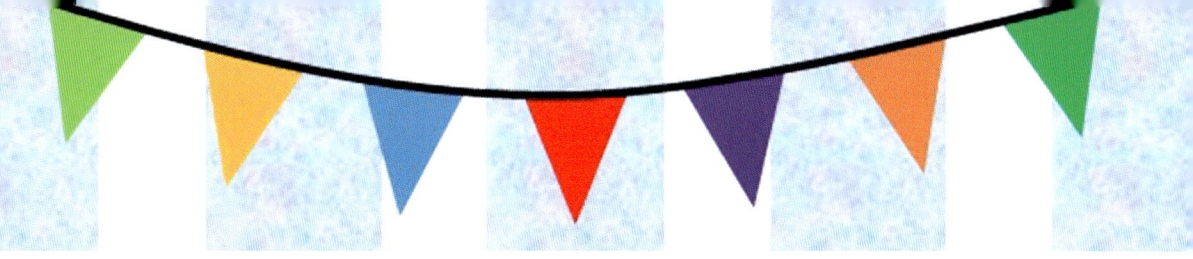

Figure 5

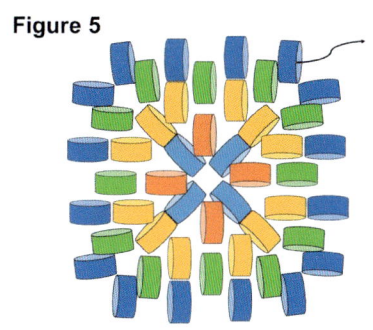

Figure 6

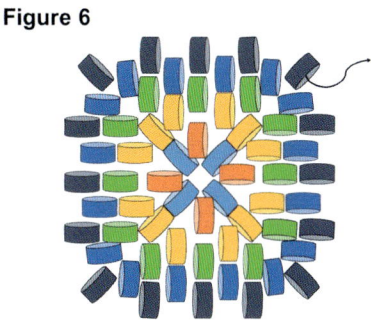

Figure 7

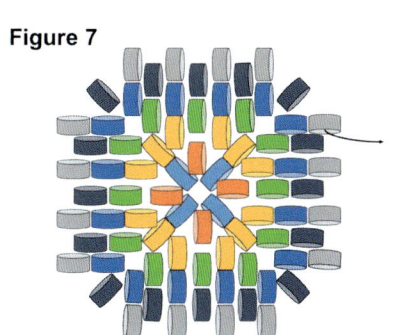

Figure 8

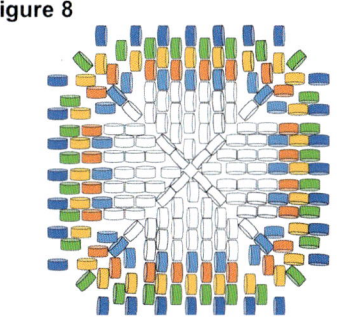

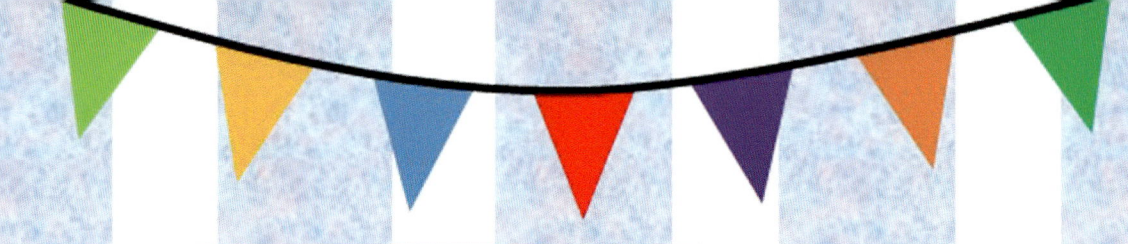

Rows 13-21: Stitch one more complete increase cycle and then the first four rows of the next (fourth) increase cycle, so you should end up with a single bead in each corner, not the large gap that you normally have at the end of an increase cycle. See figure 9.

The Back

Repeat the same 21 rows to make an identical back for your card. You then need to weave your way to the nearest corner. You are going to use the Right Angle Weave thread path to join the two halves. Although it would be possible to just zip up the two sides using an additional row of Peyote stitch, I have found that the RAW gives a flexible spine that allows the card to open and close more easily. Figure 10 shows the thread path described below.

Pass on down to exit from the first bead in your side. Pick up 1 bead and pass up through the top bead on the side of the other half of the card. Pick up 1 bead and pass down through the bead from the first half – the bead from which you started (black thread path). Pass on through the first bead you added, then down through the next bead on the side of the second half. Pick up a new bead and pass up through the next bead on the first half, then on through the horizontal bead from which you started this stitch (red thread path). Pass on down through the same (2nd) bead on the second half, then on through the bead you have just added and down through the next bead on the first half. The green arrow shows your exit. Keep repeating this sequence all the way down the side of the card. If you take a look at the photo at the start of this chapter, you should be able to see the join clearly - this may help you to understand the technique if you are confused.

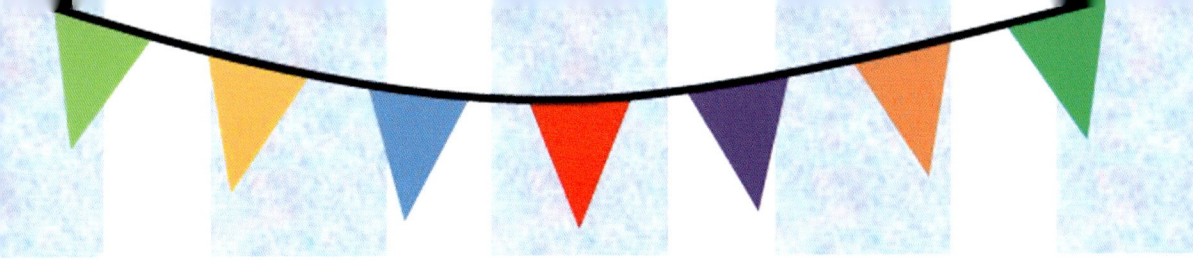

Figure 9

Figure 10

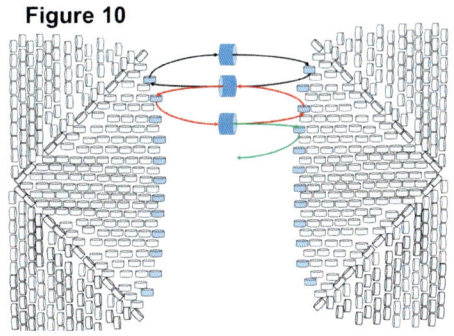

You can add some patterns into your squares. Read on to find out about some ideas and then at the end you will find a blank pattern so you can also create your own designs.

Vertical Quadrants: Stitch rows 1 and 2 in (A) beads. Then in row 3, add the first and third groups of three using (B) beads. Use (C) beads for the second and fourth groups of three and use the (A) beads for the straight edges (single beads) of the square. This sets up your patterns, so for the remaining rows, just continue to add the correct beads in the relevant places to continue this pattern.

Diagonal Quadrants: Stitch the first row in (A) beads (highlight colour), row two in (B) beads. In row 3 add 1(B), 1(A), 1(B) in each space (ie the highlight colour is the mid bead in each group of three). Rows 3 and 4, add the corner pairs in (A) and the remaining beads in (B). Row 5 stitch each corner bead in (A), the remaining beads in (B). Row 6 should be all (B) beads. Continue this pattern as you add each consecutive increase repeat.

Note: you can make the quadrants in alternate colours, so looking at the pattern, you can see the top and bottom quadrants could be stitched in one colour and the left and right quadrants stitched in the second colour (I did this for my birthday card design on page 62). To do this, every time you are stitching a row that contains (B) beads, you should add (B) along the first and third sides and then (C) along the second and fourth sides.

Outside Line: On the fourth repeat, stitch the first two rows in the contrast colour. All the other rows in this square should be stitched in the main colour.

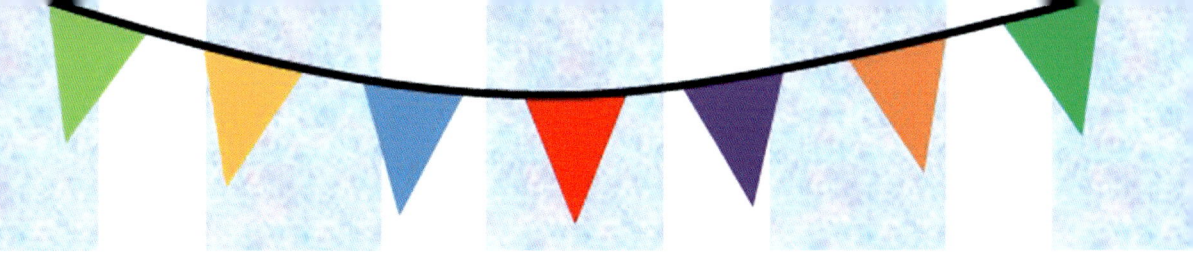

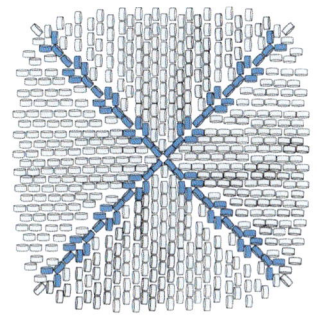

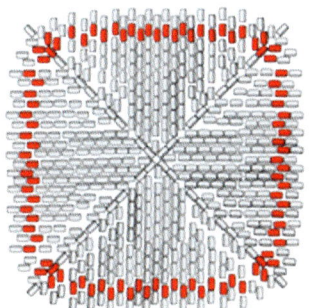

Top Left: Vertical Quadrants

Top Right: Diagonal Quadrants

Left: Outside Line

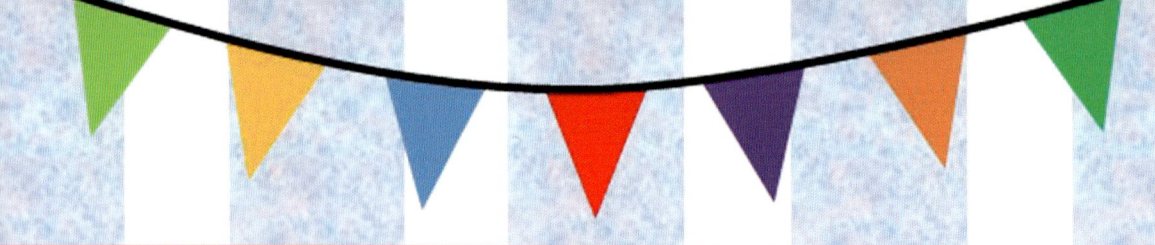

Circular Pattern

Stitch the first two rows in (A), the next two rows in colour (B), the next two rows in colour (C), the next two rows in colour (D). Repeat this sequence once and then stitch the remaining four rows in colour (C).

Floral Pattern

This starts in the second row of the third increase cycle. You will need to use colour (B) beads for the petals and colour (C) for the centre of each flower. The remaining square is stitched in (A) beads. See the pattern – you are going to add two flowers on each side.

Design Your Own

You can photocopy and enlarge the blank pattern in order to design your own variations. The projects in this book each use the variations shown, but you can of course create your own card front ideas for each type of pattern on the square card blank.

You can also use some of these pattern ideas for the backs of your square cards. I used a variation on the circular pattern when I made the Bluebell Card you can see in the gallery (page 76).

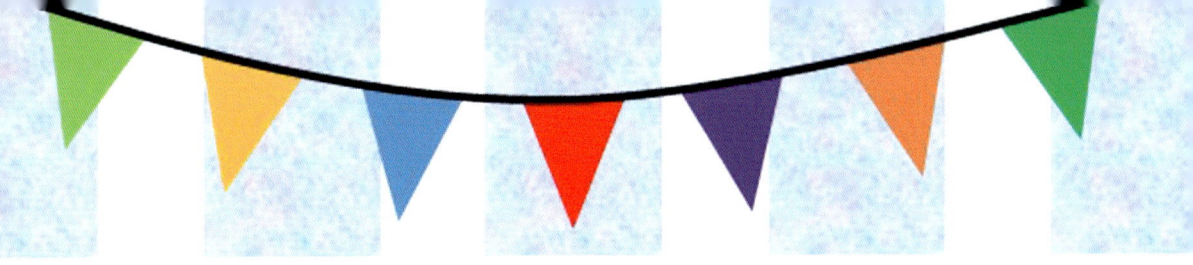

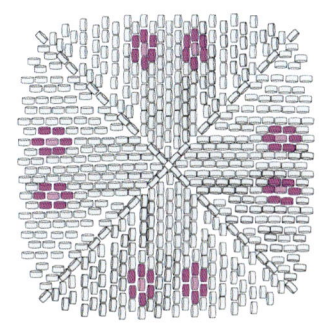

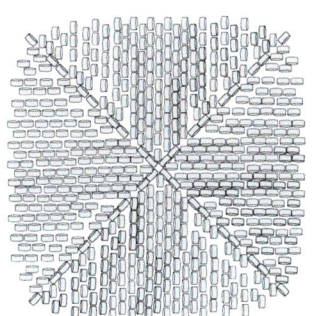

Top Left: Circular Pattern

Top Right: Floral Pattern

Left: Blank Pattern

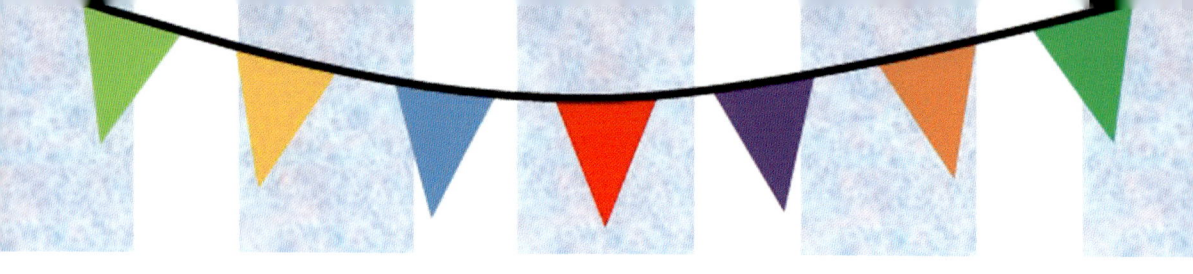

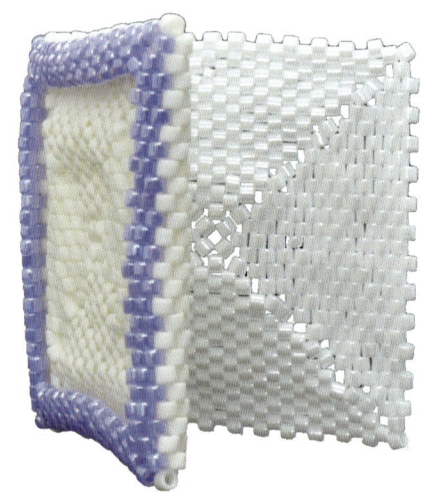

Square Aperture Card Inside

Square Aperture Card Blank

Square Aperture Card

You can add an aperture to the front of your square card blanks as well. This is done in a different way to the rectangular cards. You will continue to work in Peyote stitch, but by decreasing in the corners, you can create the aperture edging. When you first start, it may help to use a different colour of bead for the aperture so that you can see what you are doing.

Materials
13g size 10 Delicas in main colour (A)
4g size 10 Delicas in contrast colour (B)

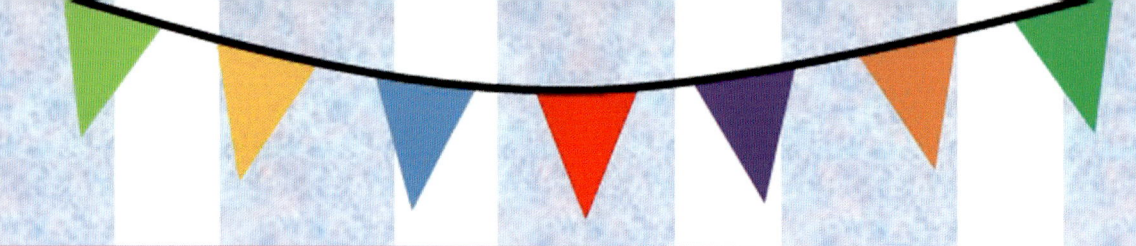

Begin by following the instructions for a square card blank to stitch the 21 rows that make the front of your card, using the (A) beads.

Row 22: Add 1(B) in each space around your card edge. See figure 1 – note, I have used a smaller square for the diagrams so you can see the new beads more clearly, but the bead count per row will not be accurate.

Row 23: add 1(B) in each space along the sides of the card, but when you reach the corner, pass through the two corner beads so that they are pulled in towards each other. You will need to pull the thread tight to ensure that the beads sit close together. This should pull your row 22 beads over to sit on the front of the card. See figure 2.

Row 24: Repeat row 23, so again you will be making a decrease in each corner and you will need to pull the thread in as tight as you can. See figure 3.

Row 25: Add 1(B) in each space, including in between the two beads in the corner. See figure 4. This is your final row, so you can finish your thread when it is complete.

Card Back: Make the basic card back by following rows 1-20 for the square card, but you are going to join this back in a different way. On the final row, add 1(A) in each space along the first two sides. When you reach the third side, instead of picking up a new bead in each space, zip the back to row 21 on the front of the card (this will be the last row of (A) beads). Then complete the final row of the back of your card and finish your thread.

Figure 1

Figure 2

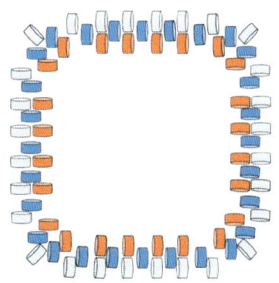

Figure 3

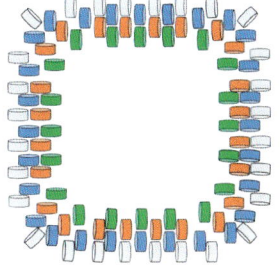

Figure 4

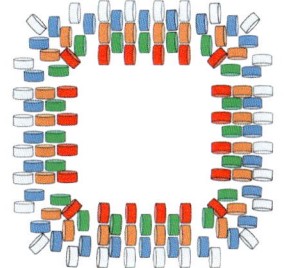

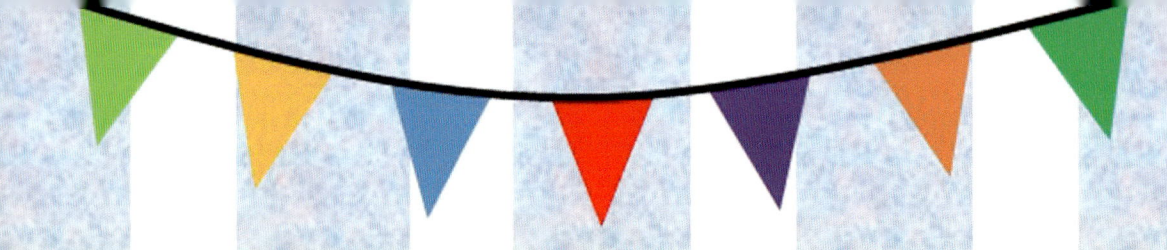

Card Front Decoration

I have decorated my card fronts with flat motifs. These are generally best made using size 10 Delicas, but you can experiment with different bead sizes and brands. Delicas will give the most regular shape, but any seed bead will work for these designs. You should just make sure that the finished design is in proportion to your card blank.

I have arranged the designs in groups according to the technique you will need to make them. Some are made in Square Stitch and some in Peyote or Brick Stitch. In some cases there is a choice, so you can use whichever technique you prefer.

When you have explored these flat patterns, you can also think about adding some three-dimensional designs to the front of your card. You will see a couple of ideas in the gallery, but have some fun creating your own too.

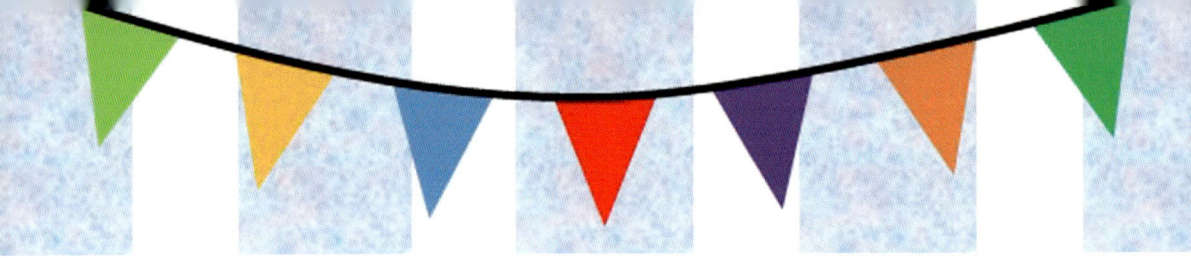

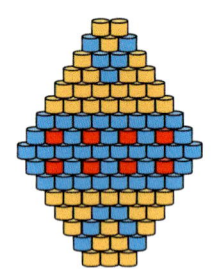

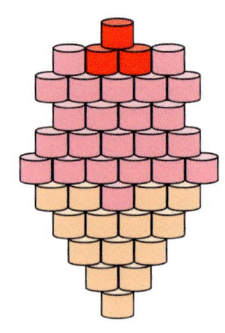

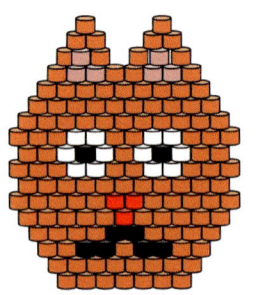

These designs are all best made in Brick Stitch.

Top Left: Easter Egg

Top Right: Ice Cream

Left: Cat Face

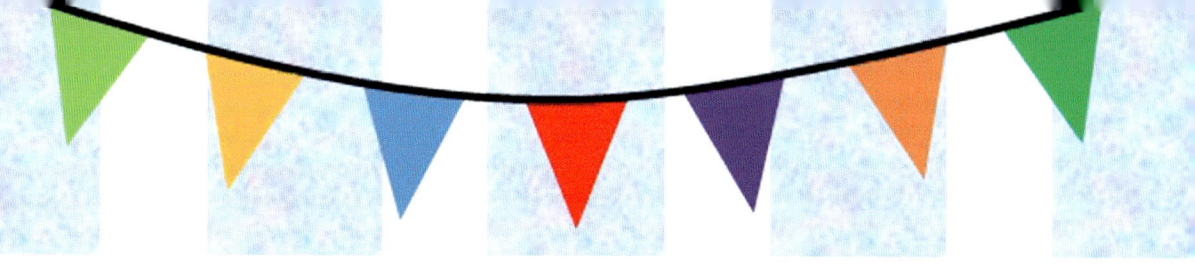

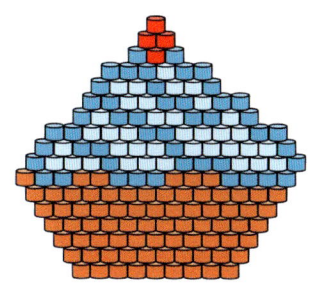

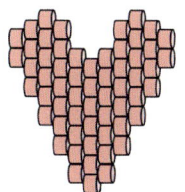

These designs are all best made in brick stitch.

Top Left: Cupcake

Top Right: Basket of Flowers

Left: Two Heart Designs

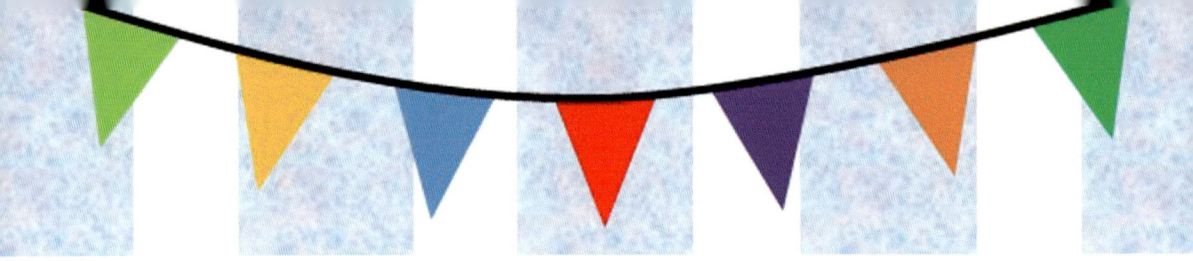

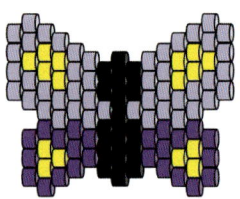

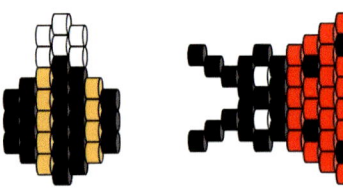

These designs can be made in Peyote Stitch or Brick Stitch. Consider which row is best to use as a starting point in order to make the pattern easy to stitch.

Top Left: Balloons
Top Right: Butterfly
Left: Insects - Bee and Ladybird

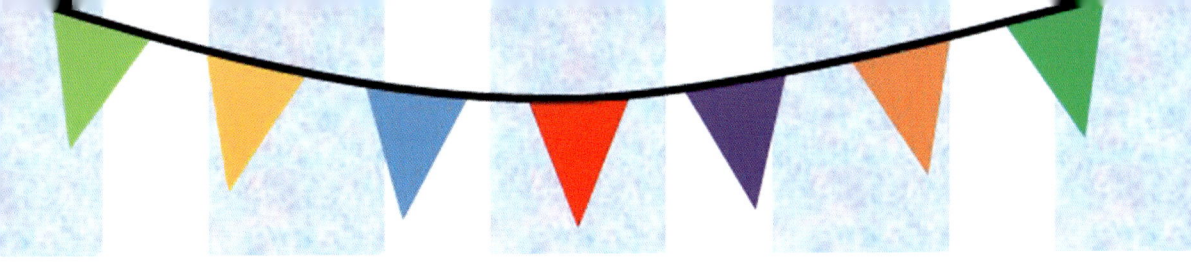

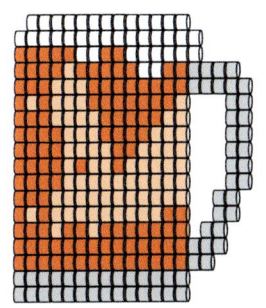

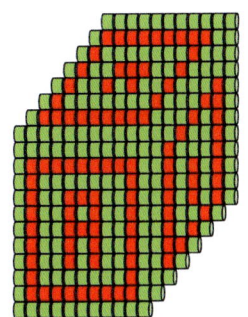

The top two designs are best made in Square Stitch. For the Christmas tree, you should work each section in brick stitch, but use square stitch to join the sections together and make the trunk.

Top Left: Beer Glass
Top Right: Baby's Block
Left: Christmas Tree

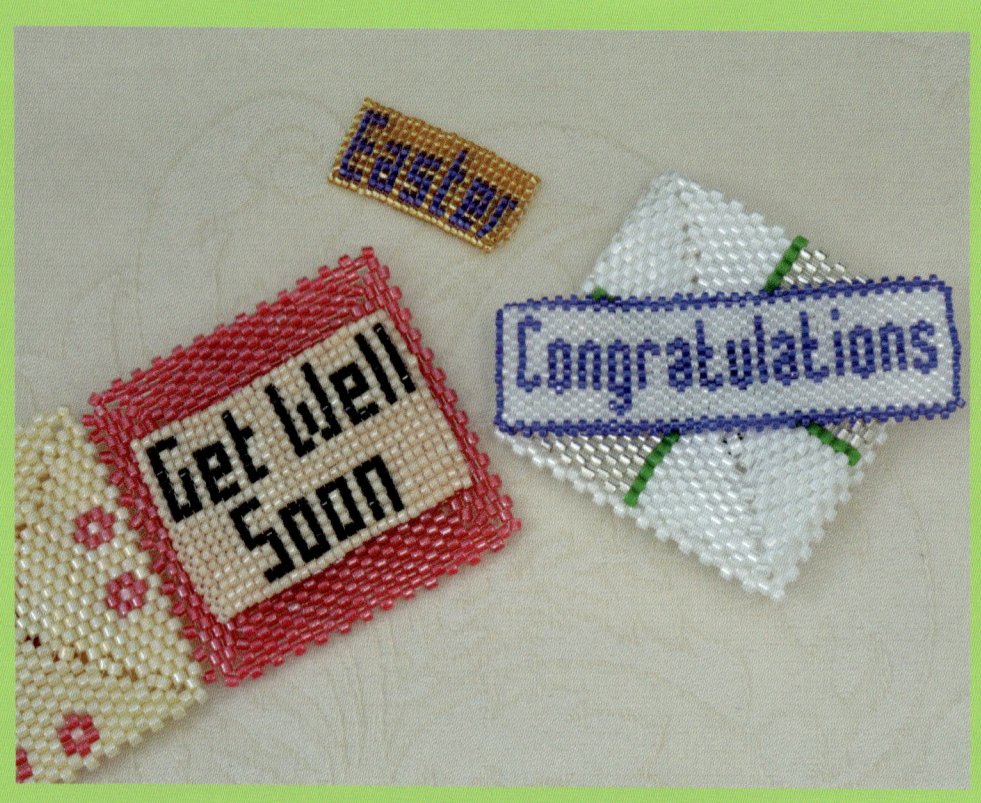

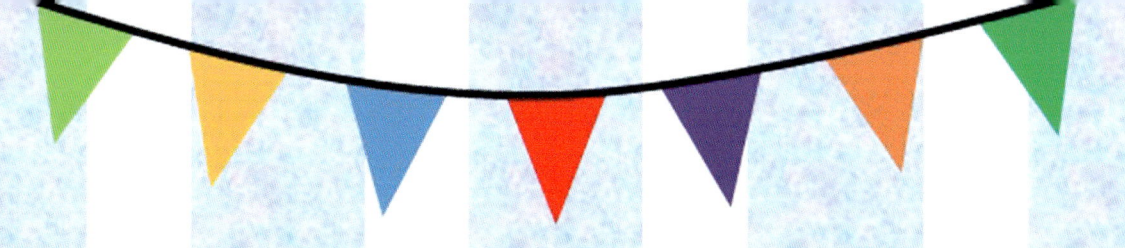

Card Messages

With some lettering you can add messages to the front or the inside of your cards. On the following pages you will find a complete alphabet and set of numbers in both Peyote stitch and Square stitch. I have also designed some greetings in each stitch which you may find useful.

Using the alphabets you can design your own greetings. You will need to make these in size 15 seed beads so that they are in proportion to your card blanks. It is a good idea to begin by making your greeting, then if it comes out too big for your card blank, you can just enlarge the card by adding some extra rows to the blank.

When you are designing your own messages, you will need to think about spacing so you ensure that the lines of text are centred or left aligned. You might also like to add borders or other small decoration to fill in gaps around the text.

Peyote Stitch Alphabet

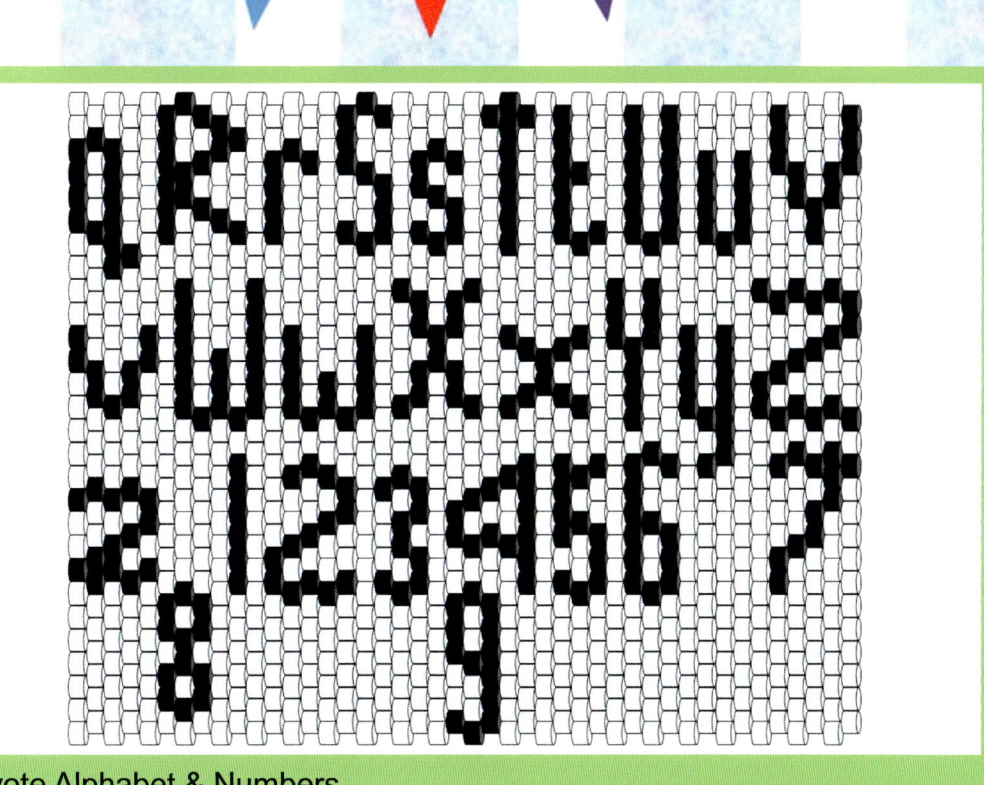

Peyote Alphabet & Numbers

You will have noticed that the Peyote alphabet and numbers can sometimes be a little uneven. I have tried to size them all so that the capital letters and small letters will sit together naturally. When you are creating a design, you will need to leave a single column of beads between each letter and then three columns of beads between each word. Try to check that you line up the new letters, so that the bottom of each letter starts on the same row. This way your greeting will sit straight across your beadwork.

I have put together some useful greetings for you, using the Peyote alphabet. You will notice that there are occasions where I have slightly altered the design of a letter (for example the 'B' for Birthday), so that it sits better with the other lettering. So, when you are creating your own designs, feel free to do this. Just try to keep the sizing even. It is also worth remembering that the way in which the eye views a beading pattern may not be as 'logical' as you think. So you may have designed the letters to match, but if you find that they look strange or uneven, do not be afraid to make small alterations in order to achieve a more uniform effect. Remember, you can also bead these designs using Brick stitch if you find that easier.

I like to maintain that there is no 'right' and 'wrong' when it comes to beading. Of course it is a good idea to learn some 'rules' and keep them in mind, but at the end of the day, the important thing is to create an attractive result. So if this means breaking a few rules along the way, then don't be afraid to do that!

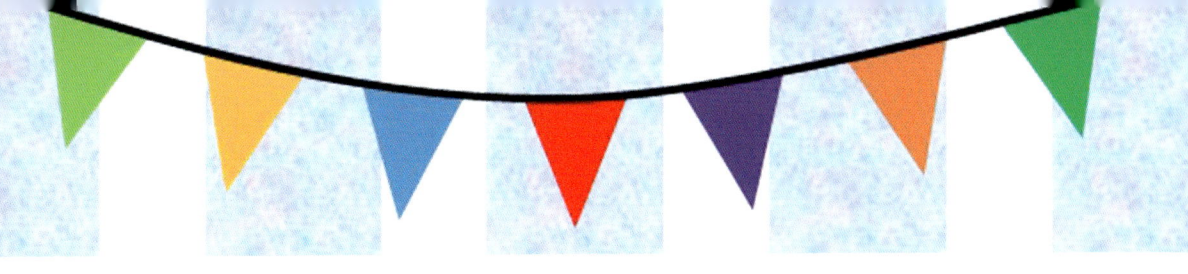

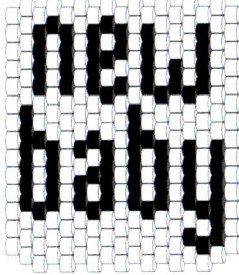

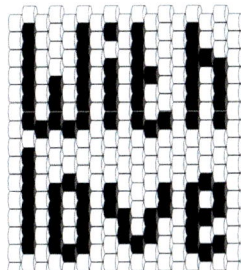

Square Stitch Alphabet

Square Stitch Alphabet & Numbers

You will have noticed that the Square Stitch alphabet and numbers are generally a lot more regular. If you compare both alphabets, you will see that some letters possibly work better in one than in the other. Unfortunately, the different stitch structure means that you cannot combine the two sets of lettering. So, if you are designing your own greeting, then think about which letters you will be using and consider which alphabet you think will look best.

You may find it a little easier to design in the Square Stitch because the beads line up more evenly. As a handy little tip, the Square Stitch designs can also be beaded using Herringbone. Although the beads sit slightly differently in the two stitches, the way in which they align (in regular columns and rows) is the same. So if you are already a fan of Herringbone, you could consider using it for your greetings.

I have designed a few different greetings using the Square Stitch alphabet. Again, you may want to make small alterations to individual letters as you create a design, so use your discretion and find what works best for you.

You will find some small blank charts in the 'Useful Stuff' section at the end of this book. You can photocopy these and enlarge them in order to create your own designs. You can also find some free beading stitch charts to download from www.beadflowers.co.uk.

Merry Christmas

Easter Blessings

Get Well Soon

For Your Wedding

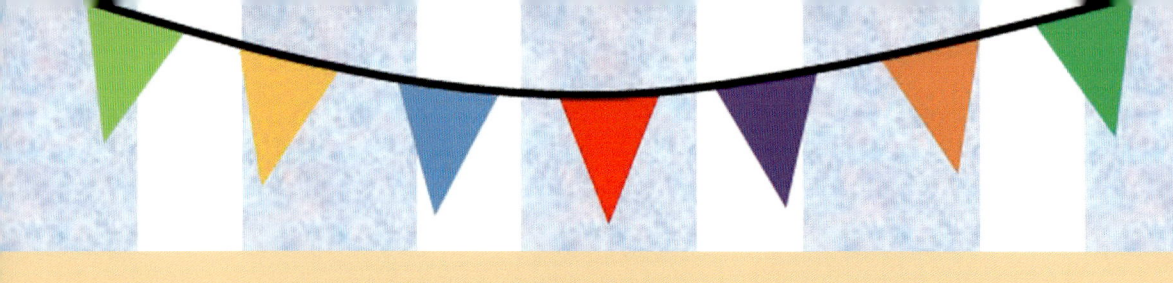

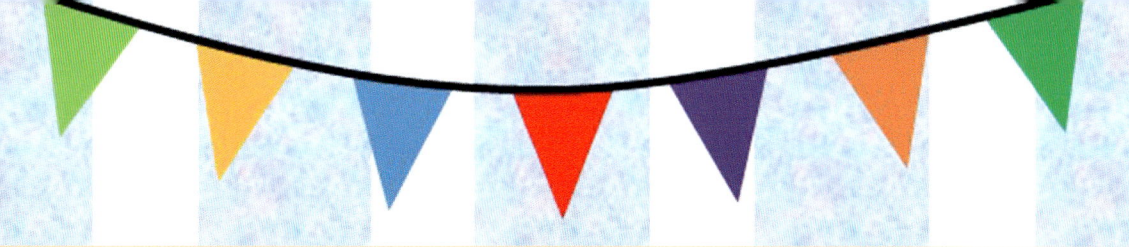

Projects

On the following pages, you will find instructions for making the cards that I designed when I was writing this book. The components of each card use design components that have been covered in earlier chapters. So, for each card, you will be shown the bead colours that I used, the card blank and then the front design and message.

If you want to familiarise yourself with the techniques, then it is a good idea to begin with one of these projects, so you can just focus on the beading by using a tried and tested design. By the time you have made a card, you will understand how everything works, so you will be ready to move on to create your own designs. This could be something as simple as changing the bead colours or mixing and matching the card front designs. Or, if you are feeling braver, then why not try creating your own front design and lettering? In the 'Useful Stuff' you will find some blank pattern paper that you can use for designing. So, have fun!

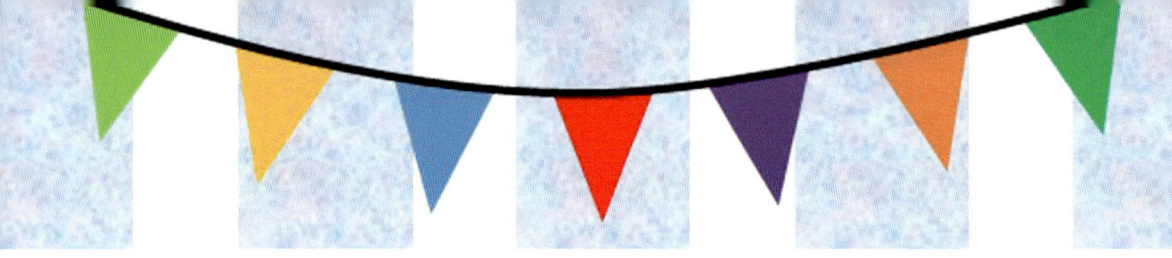

Golden Anniversary Card

- 12g size 11 Delicas DB201: Ceylon White (A)
- 1g size 11 Delicas DB042: Silver Lined Gold (B)
- 1g size 11 Delicas DB157: Cream (C)
- 1g size 11 Delicas DB272: Goldenrod Lined Topaz (D)
- 1g size 15 seed beads in Black
- Ten 4mm crystals in Gold

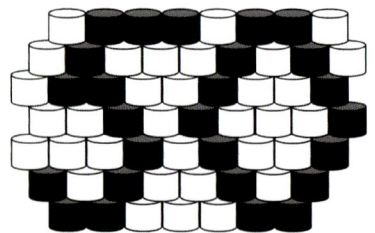

This was the original card I made to celebrate the 50th issue of Bead Magazine. You could alter the colouring and number to suit any anniversary.

Step 1: Follow the instructions to make the rectangular card blank (page 10). You will be using the (A) beads for the main card and the (B) beads for the highlight in the aperture.

Step 2: The front pattern is made using the Balloons design (page 40). You should use the (B), (C) and (D) beads to make the balloons. Then use the (A) and (B) beads to stitch the '50' from the design on the facing page. Position the '50' at the bottom of your card and stitch it in place. Position the balloons and stitch them in place, then use the (E) beads to add the strings from the balloons to the '50'. Finish the front by stitching your crystals randomly on the card.

Step 3: You could add a greeting inside the card, or just leave it blank.

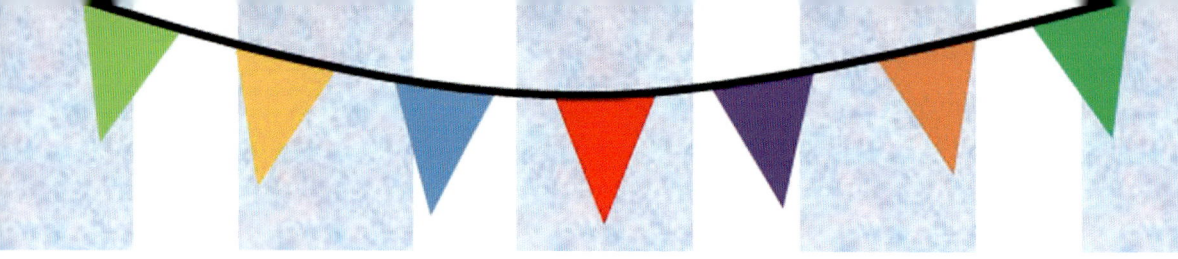

Mother's Day Card

- 12g size 11 Delicas DB353: Dark Cream Matte (A)
- 10g size 11 Delicas DB200: Opaque White (B)
- 5g size 11 Delicas DBC001: Black Hex Cut (C)
- 10g size 11 Delicas DB760: Opaque Light Sapphire (D)
- 2g size 11 Delicas DB751: Opaque Yellow (E)
- 1g size 11 Delicas DB175: Transparent Emerald AB (F)
- 5g size 11 Delicas DB724: Opaque Pea Green (G)
- 1g size 11 Delicas DB875: Mauve Opaque Lilac (H)

Make a pretty, bright card to celebrate your Mum.

Step 1: Follow the instructions to make the rectangular landscape card blank (page 18). You will be using the (A) beads for the main card and the (C) for the highlights on the aperture. You should use the (B) and (C) beads for the text and the (B) to (G) beads for the picture. The patterns for the text and picture are on the next page.

Step 2: Use the pattern for the Butterfly (page 40) and work with your (A), (C), (E) and (H) beads to make this creature. Add antennae: exit from the top of the body, pick up 5(C) and pass back down through the first four of these beads and back into the top of the body. Use the same technique to add a second antenna. Position the butterfly on the front of the card and anchor just the body onto the card, so the wings will be free to move. Finish off any loose threads and your card is complete.

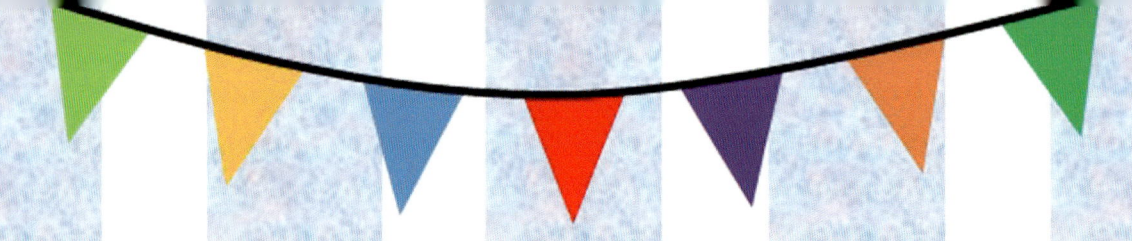

on Mother's day

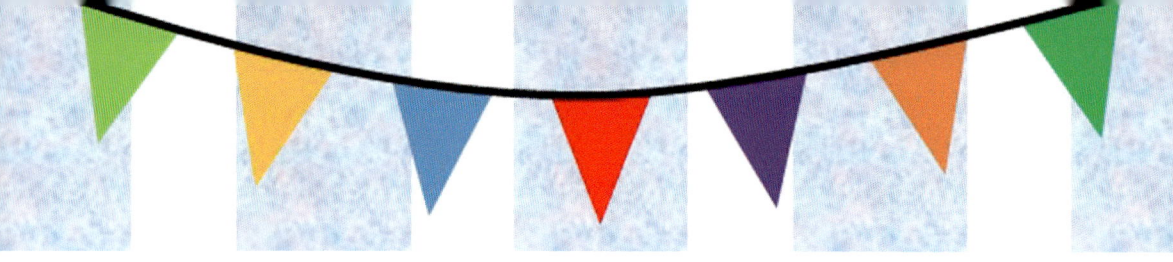

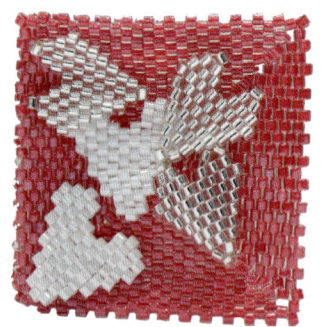

Valentine's Card

- 13g size 10 Delicas in DBM914: Sparkling Rose Lined Crystal (A)
- 2g size 10 Delicas in DBM041: Silver Lined Crystal (B)
- 2g size 10 Delicas in DBM201: Ceylon White (C)

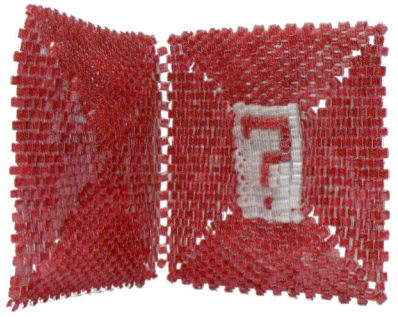

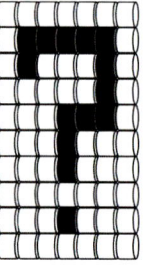

If you want a Valentine's idea that is just a little bit different, then why not make a Keepsake card?...just make sure this goes to someone special!

Step 1: Follow the instructions to make the square card blank (page 22) using the (A) beads.

Step 2: The front pattern is made using the Hearts design (page 39). You should use the (B) and (C) beads for the hearts. You could try making both designs or just use your favourite. Stitch your hearts onto the front of the card.

Step 3: Use whichever beads you like to make the '?' greeting to go inside the card. You should follow the pattern on the facing page - this is made using Square Stitch, or you can work it in Herringbone if you prefer. Stitch it to the centre inside the card. Alternatively, you could use the 'With Love' greeting, design your own personal greeting, or perhaps use something like, 'Be Mine'.

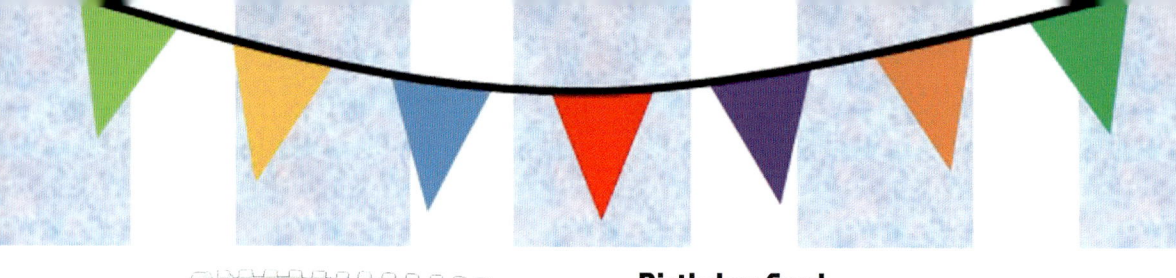

Birthday Card

- 5g size 10 Delicas in DBM177: Transparent Capri Blue AB (A)
- 10g size 10 Delicas in DBM201: Ceylon White (B)
- 5g size 10 Delicas in DBM175: Chocolate (C)
- 2g size 10 Delicas in DBM852: Matte Trans. Light Topaz AB (D)
- 2g size 10 Delicas in DBM164: Opaque Turquoise Blue AB (E)
- 4 size 11 seed beads in Red (F)
- 2g size 15 seed beads in White (G)
- 1g size 15 seed beads in Black (H)

This cute card is perfect for anyone who likes a bit of cake!

Step 1: Follow the instructions to make the square card blank (page 22) with diagonal quadrants (pages 28-29). You will be using the (A) beads for the diagonal lines, the (B) and (C) beads for the quadrants. The card back and the spine should be made with the (B) beads.

Step 2: The front pattern is made using the Cupcake design (page 39). You should use the (D) beads for the cake, the (A) and (E) beads for the icing and the (F) beads for the cherry on top. Stitch your Cupcake onto the centre front of the card, taking care that your stitching doesn't show.

Step 3: Use the (G) and (H) beads to make the greeting to go inside the card. You should follow the pattern for the Peyote Stitch 'Happy Birthday' on page 47. Finish by stitching this into the centre of the back of the card on the inside. Again, take care that your stitching does not show. Your card is now complete.

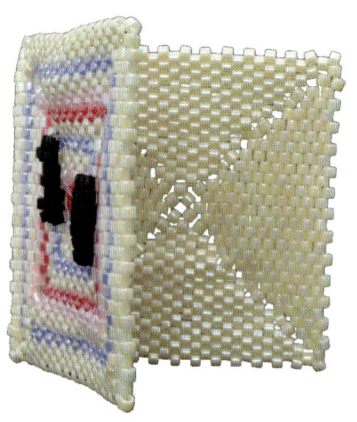

Age Card
- 2g size 10 Delicas in DBM914: Sparkling Rose Crystal (A)
- 2g size 10 Delicas in DBM055: Pink Lined Crystal AB (B)
- 10g size 10 Delicas in DBM157: Opaque Cream AB (C)
- 2g size 10 Delicas in DBM249: Purple Ceylon (D)
- 1g size 10 Delicas in DBM310: Matte Black (E)

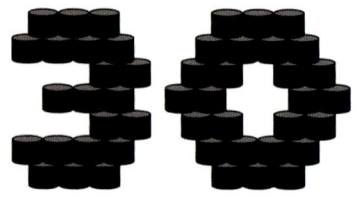

Personalise this card to commemorate a 'Special' birthday. You can use the favourite colours of the recipient and design the age for the front.

Step 1: Follow the instructions to make the square card blank (page 22) with a circular pattern (pages 29-31). You will be using the (A) to (D) beads as described in the pattern instructions. The card back and the spine should be made with the (C) beads.

Step 2: The front pattern is made from two numbers stitched onto the card. I stitched these using Brick stitch and made them so that they were self-supporting. You can see the pattern I used on the facing page. If you wish, you can design your own numbers, or you could use the number designs from the chapter on Card Messages, to make a little age plaque. When you stitch the numbers onto your card, take care that the thread does not show.

Step 3: I did not add a greeting inside this card, but you could design something appropriate.

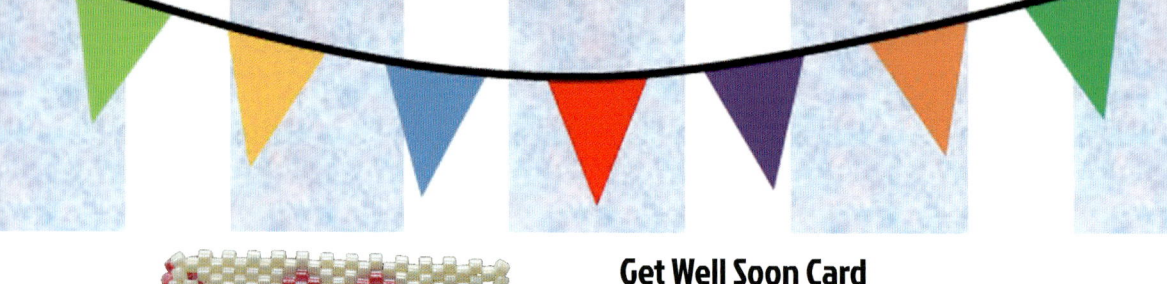

Get Well Soon Card

- 10g size 10 Delicas in DBM157: Opaque Cream AB (A)
- 10g size 10 Delicas in DBM914: Sparkling Rose Lined Crystal (B)
- 2g size 10 Delicas in DBM055: Pink Lined Crystal AB (C)
- 1g size 10 Delicas in DBM852: Matte Trans. Light Topaz AB (D)
- 8 size 10 Delicas in DBM163: Opaque Green AB (E)
- 5 size 10 Delicas in DBM053: Light Yellow S. L. Crystal (F)
- 2g size 11 Delicas in DB204: Ceylon Light Beige (G)
- 1g size 11 Delicas in DBC010: Black Hex Cut (H)

You could use this design as a birthday card or, as I did, for a get well card.

Step 1: Follow the instructions to make the square card blank (page 22) with a floral pattern (pages 30-31). You will be using the (A) to (C) beads for the patterned card front. I chose to make a contrasting card back and spine, so use the (B) beads for this.

Step 2: The front pattern is made using the Basket of Flowers design (page 39). You should use the (D) beads for the basket, the (B) and (C) beads for the flowers, with (F) bead centres and the (E) for leaves. Stitch your design onto the centre front of the card and add the basket handle as a string of 25 (D) beads anchored into place on the card.

Step 3: Use the (G) and (H) beads to make the greeting to go inside the card. You should follow the pattern for the Square Stitch 'Get Well Soon' on page 51. Finish by stitching this into the centre of the card back on the inside.

Congratulations Card

- 2g size 10 Delicas in DBM154: Opaque Green AB (A)
- 10g size 10 Delicas in DBM201: Ceylon White (B)
- 5g size 10 Delicas in DBM041: Silver Lined Crystal (C)
- 5g size 15 seed beads in White (D)
- 2g size 15 seed beads in Silver Lined Purple (E)
- 1g size 15 seed beads in Black (F)

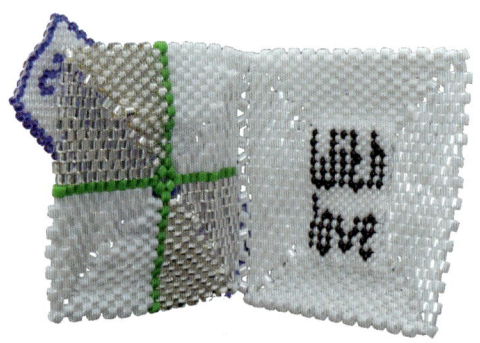

Use this design to celebrate any occasion. You can add an appropriate greeting for the inside, using my designs or one of your own.

Step 1: Follow the instructions to make the square card blank (page 22) with vertical quadrants (pages 28-29). You will be using the (A) beads for the dividing lines, the (B) and (C) beads for the quadrants. The card back and the spine should be made with the (B) beads.

Step 2: The front pattern is made using the Congratulations message from page 47. You should use the (D) beads for the background and (E) beads for lettering and border. Stitch your message across the centre front of the card, taking care that you place it so that the card will still stand up.

Step 3: Use the (D) and (F) beads to make the 'With Love' greeting to go inside the card, following the Peyote Stitch on page 47. Finish by stitching this into the centre of the card back on the inside. Your card is now complete.

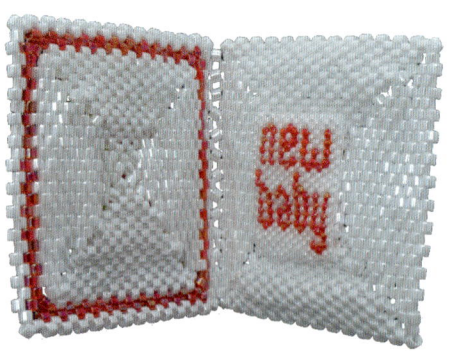

Baby Card

- 13g size 10 Delicas in DBM201: Ceylon White (A)
- 2g size 10 Delicas in DBM172: Transparent Red AB (B)
- 5g size 10 Delicas in DBM053: Transparent Yellow Lined Crystal (C)
- 2g size 15 seed beads in White (D)
- 1g size 15 seed beads in Red (E)

This design is perfect to welcome a new baby, or you could alter it to suit a Christening. Why not add the baby's name?

Step 1: Follow the instructions to make the square card blank (page 22) with an outline (pages 28-29). You will be using the (A) beads for the main card and the (B) beads for the outline. The card back and the spine should be made with the (A) beads.

Step 2: The front design is made using the Baby's Block design (page 41). You should use the (C) beads for the main block and the (B) beads for the design details. Stitch your block onto the centre front of the card, taking care that your stitching doesn't show.

Step 3: Using the (D) and (E) beads, make the 'New Baby' greeting to go inside the card (page 47). Finish by stitching this into the centre of the back of the card on the inside. Again, take care that your stitching does not show, and your card is complete.

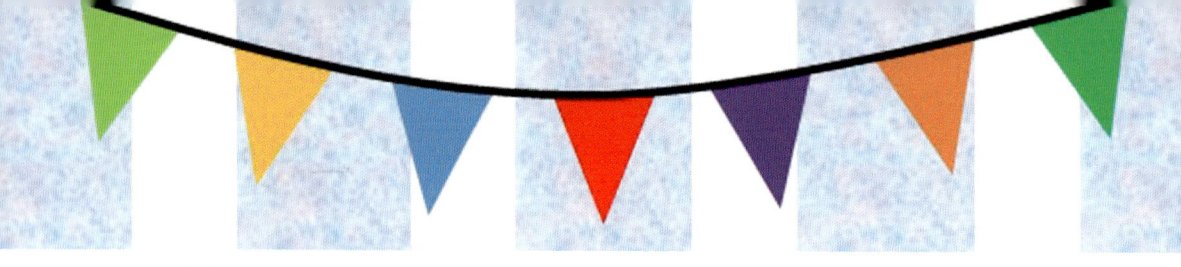

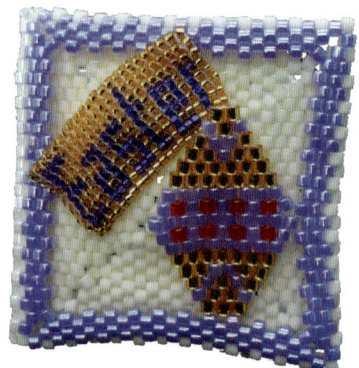

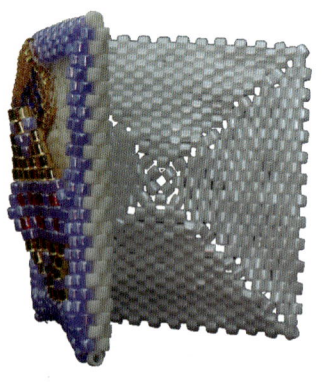

Easter Card

- 7g size 10 Delicas in DBM352: Matte Opaque Cream (A)
- 5g size 10 Delicas in DBM249: Purple Ceylon (B)
- 7g size 10 Delicas in DBM201: Ceylon White (C)
- 1g size 10 Delicas in DBM042: Silver Lined Gold (D)
- 8 size 10 Delicas in DBM172: Transparent Red AB (E)
- 1g size 15 seed beads in Silver Lined Gold (F)
1g size 15 seed beads in Silver Lined Purple (G)

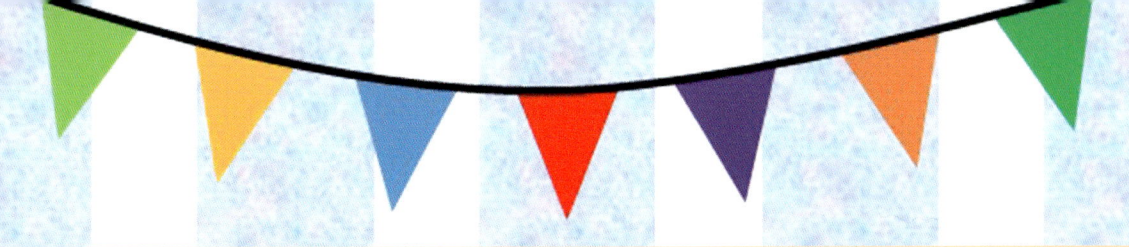

Step 1: Follow the instructions to make the square aperture card blank (page 34). You will be using the (A) beads for the main card front and the (B) beads for the aperture. The card back is made with the (C) beads.

Step 2: The front pattern is made using the Easter Egg design (page 38). You should use the (B), (D) and (E) beads for the design. Stitch your motif onto the front of the card, anchoring it along the top of the aperture edge - you can just stitch the bottom of the egg to hold it in place.

Step 3: Use the (F) and (G) beads to make the front wording. You should follow the pattern for the Square Stitch 'Easter Blessings' on page 51, but just stitch the word 'Easter'. Add this to the front of the card - position it where you wish and then anchor it into place, taking care that your stitching does not show. This completes my design, but you could add your own greeting to the inside if you wish.

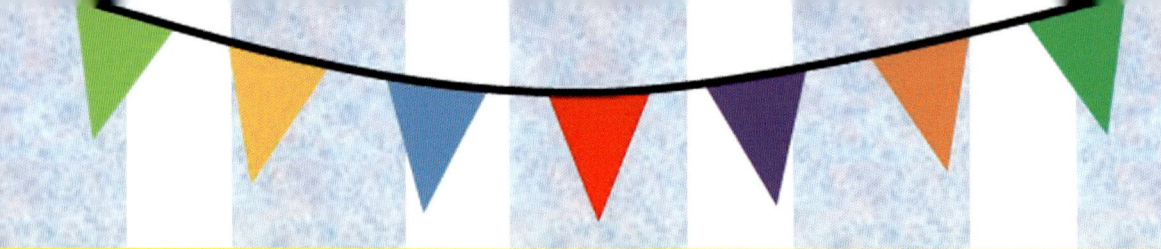

Gallery

On the following pages you can find some more inspirational ideas. These are all projects that use the techniques you have learned in this book, but develop them in different ways. I have described what I did for each project so that you can also try your own versions if you wish. In some cases the project is available as a separate pattern on my website, so if you want to try it for yourself, then I have included the details where you can find the pattern.

Some of the projects are designs that I created for competitions, so they were simply too large and complex to write up. I also like to keep some of my work just for my own personal enjoyment, so it is often a conscious decision to make something for which I will never write a tutorial. I wanted to include these projects because I wanted you to see just how much potential the Keepsake Cards idea has. If you take this further and develop your own designs and ideas, I would love to hear about them.

Christmas Decoration

I adapted the rectangular card blank to make a simple Christmas decoration. If you simply stitch 46 rows, instead of 92, then make the aperture section in the same way, you can fold the aperture over to create just the 'front' of a card. I used size 11 Delicas to make the Christmas tree design (page 41) and stitched it to the front of the card. I used a 4mm bicone to add a star to the top of the tree and a combination of Tilas, Cubes and size 8 seed beads to add parcels at the bottom of the tree.

At the moment the back of the card is blank, but you could design a decoration to stitch on that side as well (or perhaps a name to personalise it).

Finish it up with a piece of ribbon on the top and hang it on a Christmas tree. I know that a lot of people like to make special decorations, so this would be a great way to create something really special, or maybe to mark a memorable Christmas.

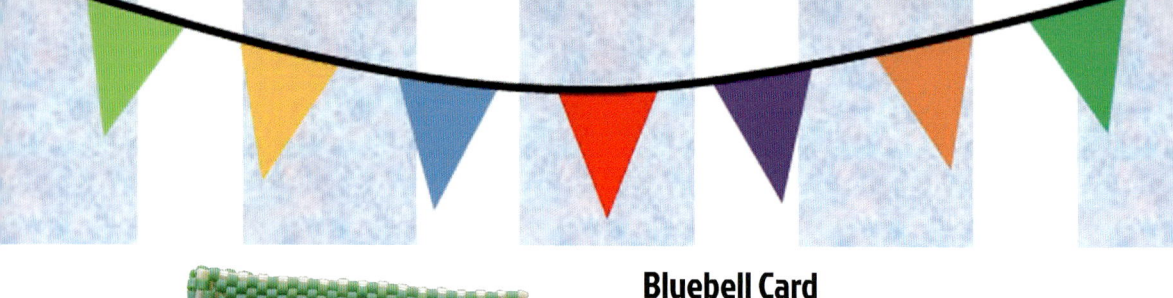

Bluebell Card

This is a version of the Square Aperture card, but I added some three-dimensional bluebells to the front. I had to stitch an extra increase cycle to fit my bluebells. The flowers were made from size 15 seed beads and worked in circular and tubular Herringbone (Row 1: 3 beads. Row 2: increase to 6 beads. Row 3: increase to 9 beads. Row 4: increase to 12 beads. Rows 5-10: 12 beads per row. Row 11: use 1 bead in each stitch).

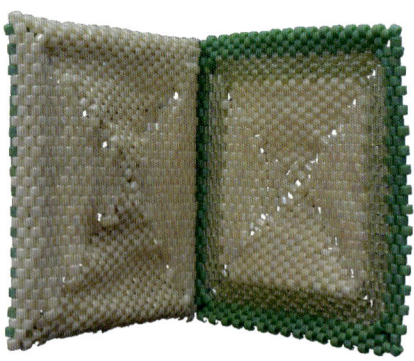

I then stitched the bluebells onto the card, adding a stem using the same green beads that I had used for the aperture. I finished the design by dotting size 15 beads over the card front. I used one of the pattern designs for the card back. This idea would work with other miniature flowers as well.

Locket

In another adaptation of the Square aperture idea, I made this locket with a three-dimensional heart on the front. It's perfect for carrying around photos of those you love. The back of the locket incorporates a pattern and is made using straight Peyote, so you really get to test your bead-weaving techniques with this design.

The full pattern is available on my website, so if you want to give it a go, find it at www.beadflowers.co.uk

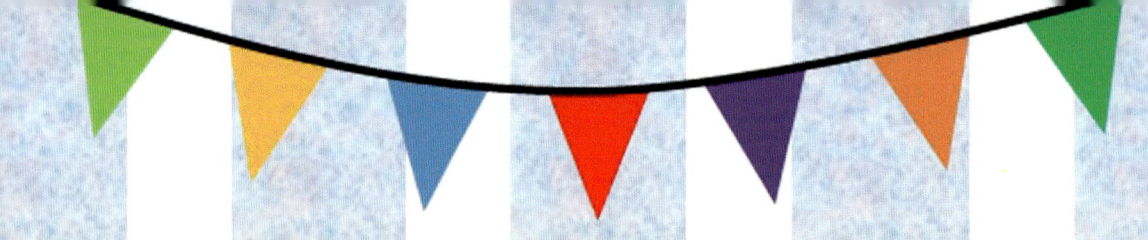

Beaded Books

Both these beaded books were made for competitions. The little blue book was the first that I made and it was the first time that I really started exploring the ideas that have gone into this Keepsake Cards project. The competition was run by Beadwork Magazine back in 2009 and it was themed, 'The Beaded Book.' So, I decided to take the theme literally and make a book out of beads. I designed the pictures and words that I wanted to use, then realised that they would need to be made in really tiny beads to look right. So the entire book was made from size 15 seed beads. The book was judged as one of the winners, so it travelled to the USA to go on display at Beadfest, but it did not win the overall prize.

In 2013, as I was trying to come up with an idea for the British Bead Awards, I was also exploring the beaded cards idea further and had developed the ideas for creating apertures. I decided to try another beaded book, but this time, the pages included cut out sections that allowed me to incorporate lots of shaped beads to create three-dimensional designs. Again, I worked in Peyote stitch to create the pages: each page had a front and back (like the card fronts and backs), but joined to form a single page. I then joined all the pages to one another down the spine of the book, made a front and back cover, then used Herringbone to create a flexible spine to cover the stitching and allow the pages to be turned. This book also reached the finals of the competition, but did not win any prizes!

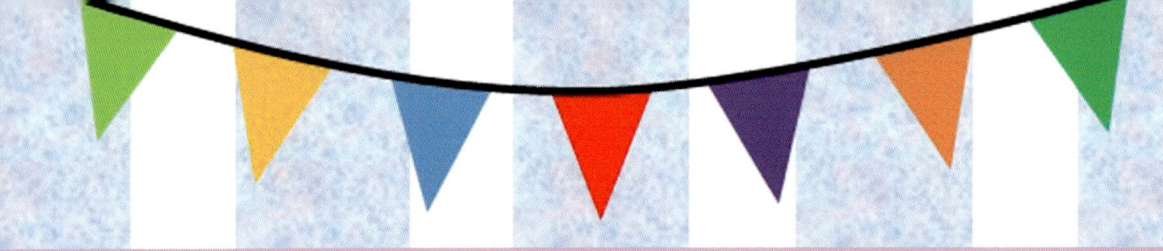

Useful Stuff

If you want to try designing your own patterns, then you can photocopy and enlarge the graph paper on the facing page.

The beads I have used for this book have been purchased from three of my favourite bead shops. Charisma Beads are a Delica bead specialist and have the best range of size 10 Delicas that I know of in the UK. GJ Beads and Stitchncraft are both brilliant bead shops with great customer service. You can buy size 11 Delicas and a whole range of other beads from both of them.

Charisma Beads www.charismabeads.co.uk
GJ Beads www.gjbeads.co.uk
Stitchncraft www.stitchncraft.co.uk

If you want help with techniques, then you can download free tutorials from www.beadflowers.co.uk - just search through the Free Tutorials section on the website. If you want to know more about the materials, techniques, or general beading advice, then go and explore www.myworldofbeads.com where I have a lot of blogs covering all aspects of beading. If you go straight to the Index page then you can see a full list of blog posts and pages, so you should be able to find what you are looking for. If you cannot find it, then do feel free to get in touch with me for more help.

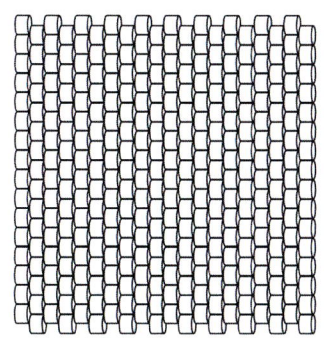

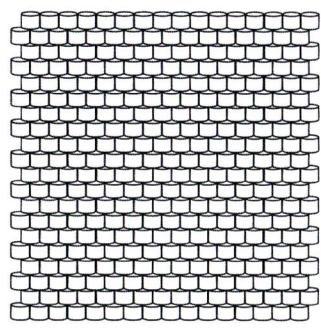

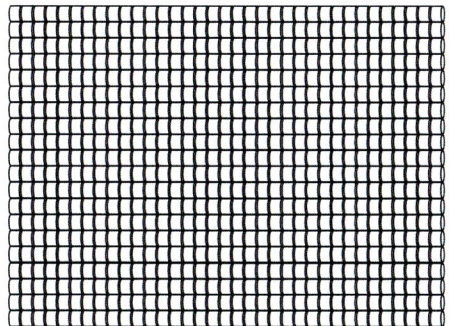

Top Left: Peyote Stitch

Top Right: Brick stitch

Left: Square Stitch

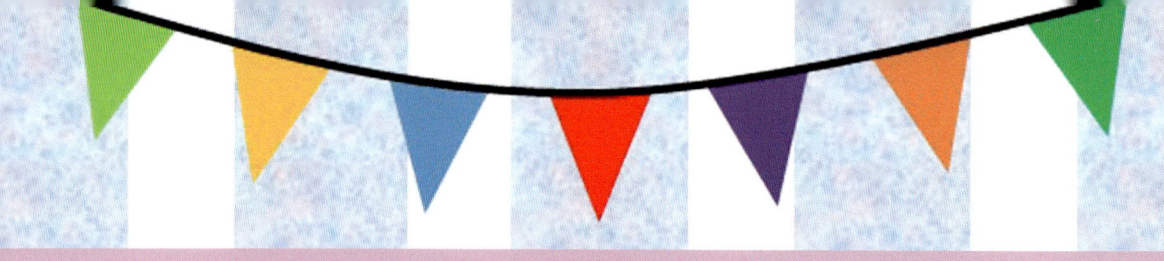

Katie Dean is a self-taught bead artist who began beading in 2003. Her designs have been published in beading magazines throughout the world. She has been a finalist or winner in several international beading competitions. She has worked as editor of Bead and Jewellery Magazine, appeared on The Craft Channel, worked as a guest designer for Jewellery Maker TV and works for the Beadsmith Inspiration Squad.

Katie is a qualified teacher and teaches beading at classes around the UK. This is her tenth beading book. To find out more about Katie's work and teaching schedule, please visit her website, www.beadflowers.co.uk.